GOD
and the
AQUARIAN
AGE

The new era of the Kingdom

ADRIAN B. SMITH

McCRIMMONS
Great Wakering Essex

First published in 1990 by McCrimmon Publishing Co. Ltd.
10-12 High Street Great Wakering Essex

ISBN 0 85597 448 6

Cover: Paul Foakes
Typeset and printed by Permanent Typesetting & Printing Ltd

GOD
and the
AQUARIAN
AGE

'The Church's mind and heart turn to the Holy Spirit as this twentieth century draws to a close.'

'The Church is also responding to certain deep desires which she believes she can discern in people's hearts today: a fresh discovery of God in his transcendent reality as the infinite Spirit;...the need to adore him in spirit and truth; the hope of finding in him the secret of love and the power of a 'new creation'...

'The Church feels herself called to this mission of proclaiming the Spirit, while together with the human family she approaches the end of the second Millennium after Christ.'

(Encyclical Letter of Pope John Paul II on the Holy Spirit. May 1986. Nos. 49, 2)[1]

[1]*Published in England by the Catholic Truth Society, London*

Contents

Foreword

It is obvious that the world is now entering into a new era, and the reluctance of many to commit themselves to the institutional Churches is a sign as well as a symptom of this change. At the same time there is a god-shaped vacuum in the souls of multitudes, and they are looking for a spirituality appropriate for today which does not mean jettisoning their Christian past.

It is to this situation that Fr. Adrian Smith, by reading the 'signs of the times', addresses himself in *God and the Aquarian Age*. It is possible to feel deeply grateful for what he writes here without necessarily accepting all his ideas — for example, the astrology implicit in the title. Fr. Smith is a loyal member of his Church, but here he rightly gives priority to God's Kingdom. This is a refreshing work, showing a spiritual largeness and freedom without abandoning the author's Christian commitment. There is discernment in its spirituality, and a welcome emphasis on the power of prayer and meditation.

This is a book which opens up new dimensions, preferring a more holistic and intuitive approach to the intellectualism of past theology. I cannot pretend that I found myself accepting all its ideas, but I am really grateful for it, because I was spiritually warmed and enriched by reading it; and I hope that others will have the same experience.

Bishop Hugh Montefiore

Introduction

My personal vocation in life is to be a missionary. I have been following this calling for the past forty years. During that time it has taken different forms according to the nature of the work and the geographical place to which my superiors have appointed me. But it has also taken different forms according to the way in which, as the years have passed, I have understood the meaning of the 'Good News' which it has been my missionary task to proclaim. To be a missionary, to participate in and to continue the missionary task given to Jesus by God, is to be, as he was, a proclaimer of the Good News.

In essence, the Good News today is the same as that proclaimed by Jesus. Namely, that God is active at each moment of the world's history in bringing about his design. The form of that Good News — the proclamation of *how* God is active — differs from one period of history to another according as the world and God's design evolve. By reading the 'signs of the times' (in the Biblical sense of signs of God's activity in history, in events) each generation perceives the form of that Good News for its own day.

In these pages I am attempting to fulfil my missionary vocation: to read the signs of our own times and to draw therefrom what is the Good News for us today. I interpret from these signs that God is doing something new among us, inviting us to enter a New Age, an age of a new God-humanity relationship, promised long ago by Jesus, but for which humanity is only now sufficiently mature in consciousness to be able to accept: the Age of the Spirit.

However, since the signs are of God's action in and with the community of humankind, no purely personal interpretation could claim authenticity, unless it were the articulation of a wider experience. I believe this to be the case. In recent years I have met an increasing number of people — and I refer to Christians, since their interpretation is being made in the light of Christian Revelation — who are arriving at the same understanding of the significance of current events and trends in our world.

The authority of this interpretation, therefore, is none other than the degree to which the reader accepts it as an authentic expression of truth because it resonates with his/her own experience.

1. The New Picture

Piecing together a jig-saw puzzle is an outworn metaphor for the task of making sense of our present world scene.

But here is a variation which I hope is more helpful. Imagine a two-sided jig-saw puzzle. Imagine too that the original box was long ago discarded so we have lost those helpful pictures of the completed puzzle. However, as we start putting pieces together we begin to realise that there is a familiarity about the picture: it is an old Master. Let us call this the Classical Picture. Other pieces, however, definitely do not sit comfortably with the old Master — the shape of the lines, the colours, the texture, the brush strokes belong to a different style. As we fit these latter pieces together, we begin to notice that nevertheless there is some similarity with the Classical Picture: that it is in fact a modern version of the same theme. Let us call this the New Picture.

Much as we may love the Classical Picture of our world, as familiar to us as the items of furniture of our childhood home, and as re-assuring, we cannot now ignore the New Picture and the way in which its 'pieces' keep intruding upon our lives, threatening to replace the former. Let us look more closely at some of these pieces.

There are the ecological pieces which tell of the polluting of rivers, lakes and seas. They picture the hacking down of tropical rain forests at the rate of 100 acres a minute, the damage to the ozone layer and the destruction of our environment caused by artificial fertilisers, pesticides, the dumping of chemical and nuclear waste, the effects of sulphorous fumes and acid rain. But they speak too of our acquiring a global vision which enables us to feel increasing concern for the ruination of our world home.

There are the pieces which picture our human condition, our planetary population which recently topped the five billion mark and is increasing rapidly; the quality of life which allows millions of children to die each year from hunger, malnutrition and related causes — in Africa alone five million children starve to death each year. The pieces reveal the hundred million people world-wide who have no home or shelter each night. But also they picture the increasing awareness of the more fortunate among us that this is our problem too because we are part of one human family, and the magnificant personal generosity to remedy the situation.

The pieces compare the needs of the world's thirteen million refugees with the £1¼ million the West spends every minute on weapons to destroy ourselves and of the many expressions of anger at the evil of this imbalance.

For us who are Christians there are pieces of the New Picture which contradict that part of the Classical Picture which we have accepted unquestioningly. In the area of Church life we had come to depend on a stability which gave us assurance amidst a rapidly changing life scene. The Church was so certain of 'truth'. Why are so many beliefs now being challenged? There is a polarisation to 'right' or to 'left' among those who claim to be loyal Christians. If the Church is really God's instrument in witnessing his revelation to the world, why is she so powerless to effect change; how do the Bob Geldofs of our time succeed in stirring the consciences of millions whilst Church leaders seem so uninspired? The way the Gospel message is presented seems to lack bite and the worship that derives from it appears so unrelated to what is really going on.

The Classical Picture enabled us to be sure of where we stood. Everything was presented in black and white; grey areas were unacceptable. There was an authority figure in State and Church who represented a Tradition, who upheld customs, upon whom we could rely for direction. The New Picture seems to have been influenced by Einstein's relativity theory. What he introduced into physics — that the measurements of speed, distance and time are variable, depending on our point of view — seems to have invaded our intellectual and moral life. There is a growing acceptance that even truth is relative, dependent on the way we perceive it. Grey areas in matters of belief have come to be acceptable.

The New Picture contains pieces which challenge moral authority. We notice that people — including ourselves perhaps — are less prepared to accept to be told what to do, how to behave, what to believe. The authority figure who told us what is right and what is wrong — from 'Daddy knows best' to 'The Pope says so, therefore....' — is losing stature. People want to make their own decision, a decision which is 'real'. It is 'real' if it is their own and relates to their reality — the context and experience of their lives. The authority of Authority is being questioned, as much within the Church as outside.

The Classical Picture was static, with God — or rather a certain concept of God as the one-time Creator — governing all things. But God was outside the picture, setting the rules, determining the laws and each piece had a pre-determined place. Provided the pieces interlocked correctly the picture was assured its survival — till the end of the world.

The New Picture is dynamic. The pieces seem to be less fixed once and for all, more adaptable, searching for new ways of understanding their contribution to the whole, wanting to have a say in what the total picture should be and less sure of the final outcome.

This New Picture may have come to our notice only comparatively recently, in the last decades, but it is in fact the product of a growing movement over the last few centuries. It is the outcome of a developing human consciousness. The first signs were noticeable already in the 16th century. Up to that time, since the beginning of the Christian era, humankind's thinking about the origin, nature and purpose of the universe was dominated in Western Europe by Church teaching — some would say by Church control. This began to be challenged in the 16th century when Copernicus and Galileo put an end to a world view that our earth was at the centre of the whole of creation. Then with the beginnings of modern science in the 17th century and the supremacy given to human reason over all other forms of knowledge in the 18th — that period of European history we call the Enlightenment — Theology and Science took their separate and independent ways.

Theology, the interpretation of reality in the light of divine Revelation, the prerogative of the Church, was largely responsible for the appearance of the Classical Picture. It was often forgotten, however, that Revelation is not the pure voice of God in a vacuum but a particular interpretation of the human story, under divine guidance, which is lived out in human history and has to be understood and expressed within the bounds of human experience, and therefore always has cultural limitations. We can only know God and the divine purpose through the same mental process by which we are able to know ourselves and our world. There is not one mental process for knowing God and another for knowing what he has created. The one and only process is by self-reflection, the human capacity that distinguishes us from animals. Consequently our understanding of the God-humanity relationship and of God's design for creation develops as human consciousness deepens.

It is the development of modern Science that has been largely responsible for the emergence of the New Picture, the new world view. Its objective study of measurable facts, providing us with a rational exploration of cause and effect, could not accept that the nature of the universe was a religious issue. While these two sources of knowledge have been following parallel paths, each rejecting and even battling against the other for the last three centuries, a third source of knowledge has become prominent in the New Picture: the knowledge of the mystic.

Older, in fact, than the other two — going back to the origin of the self-reflective human being — Mysticism has never sat at ease with either Theology or Science. Because Mysticism employs a different tool. While both Theology and Science are the product of the rational mind, Mysticism is the experience, in the intuitive mind, of direct contact with ultimate reality in its unity.

What we notice in the New Picture now is that the theological, the scientific and the mystical ways of knowing are drawing together, each realising that there exists a unity and inter-connectedness of all being, to the understanding of which each has a unique contribution to make.

I suggest that this last feature of our New Picture is the most fundamental difference with the Classical. It is a new way of knowing. And because it is a new way of knowing, a new consciousness, and not simply access to more knowledge, it colours everything else in human life, the very evolution of human life.

I mentioned earlier, when introducing the metaphor, that the New Picture was not entirely unfamiliar. This is because, for all the perplexity it causes us, it resonates with a deep human longing; it moves us towards an ideal. People of every race and culture, because of their very humanity and despite geographical and historical conditioning, have the same deepest aspirations — not in the realm of 'having' but of 'being'. Not only does the New Picture seem to respond to these deepest needs but it is the product of humanity's journey towards their fulfilment.

Some of the elements of the New Picture that I have already listed appear to be negative, devaluing humanity and our environment rather than promoting them. This, as we shall see in a later chapter, is the re-bound resulting from humanity taking a great evolutionary leap forward. Not a biological leap, this time, but a leap in consciousness. It so happens that its timing corresponds with our planet's passing from the two thousand year period of the Age of Pisces into the Aquarian Age.

It is the purpose of this book to articulate the characteristics of the New Picture and to try to understand its implications for the Christian.

I divide the book into three parts. In Part One I will be analysing the pieces of the puzzle around us and trying to see what overall pattern emerges. As Christians we have a vision against which to interpret what we see. Jesus the Christ manifested God's great design for humanity, and indeed for all creation, in the symbolism of the Kingdom of God. I shall argue that the great leap forward at this present time into the New Age of Consciousness — the Aquarian Age, as astrologers call it — should be interpreted by Christians as a major step of humanity towards the fulness of the Kingdom, a passing into the Age of the Spirit.

In Part Two I will explore the consequences of this as it affects religion, the future of the Church and our understanding of some fundamental Christian truths.

To return to our metaphor of the two-sided jig-saw puzzle, we notice that whichever picture we adopt as satisfying our need to give meaning to life the pieces all fit into the same frame. Either way we still live in the same world. The difference between the Classical and the New Pictures is not in the subject but in how we see, interpret, experience and understand the subject. And we are part of that subject, part of the picture. So our response to our understanding will affect the picture, will affect the future of our world.

The future does not just happen by accident. It is caused. Two major agents form our future. The first is the evolutionary dynamism of our planet with which we human beings are free to live in harmony or to oppose. To go along with it is to tap its energy for our well-being. To oppose it is not to obstruct its dynamism but to destroy ourselves because our very nature is a part of it. In theological terms we call this movement towards fulfilment God's Will. The second agent is free human choice. We, alone of all creatures on the earth, are free to plan and bring about our own future.

Part Three will consider this personal element, our own spiritual journey. Most of us at present are at the stage of handling pieces of the jig-saw, some of which belong to the Classical Picture and some to the New. But as we match them together there comes a moment when we have to decide to commit ourselves to adopt one world scene or the other. Only this way comes peace of mind and new energy. Once the decision is taken, all the other pieces fit together and make sense.

It is my hope that these pages will provide an interpretation of the New Picture which will facilitate the making of that decision. Our starting point, as Christians, is to reflect on God's design for humanity as we find it revealed in the pages of Scripture. Only against this revelation can we decide whether the New Picture is in keeping with, or contrary to, that design.

Part One

The signs of the times

Part One sets the scene and gathers the facts for our exploration in Part Two.

Readers will detect that I write with a bias; not with a complete disinterestedness or objectivity. First, because I am part of what is being examined. Secondly, because my fundamental belief is not only that God has a vision, a dream in his creating act, which is for our ultimate human fulfilment, but that he invites us to bring it about in partnership with him.

2. The Kingdom of God as the symbol of God's design for his creation

The Gospel is the Good News about what human life is destined to become. Although the whole of creation has been moving towards the fulfilment of God's design since its inception, it was only after several million years, with the coming among us of the Christ, that human consciousness became aware of God's design. God's vision for humanity was revealed for us in the life and teaching of Jesus (Ephesians 3:5–6). He revealed it to us in terms of 'The Kingdom of God'. Not only were almost all his parables about the Kingdom, but, more important, his whole way of living, his moral values, his ways of relating to God and to people were evidence of a new style of living which he proposed to all he encountered — and through them to all humanity. He enacted the Kingdom by the way he lived.

In terms of the biblical concept of the Kingdom of God Jesus was announcing a new era for humanity. In today's language he might have spoken instead of the Christ Age or the Age of Universality, or the New Civilisation of Love. These are all much more meaningful terms to us in a world where few kingdoms remain and even these do not provide us with an imagery which is very helpful in trying to understand what Jesus was referring to when he spoke about the reign of God as the Kingdom of God. But we will stay with that expression because it has deep biblical roots and it is through God's dealings with his people as related in the pages of the Bible that we come to understand what God's design for humanity is.

Since this design goes back to the first act of creation it is misleading to speak of Jesus as inaugurating the Kingdom. He did not inaugurate it, he manifested it. But why, we are compelled to ask, in the two million years or more of human history, has humanity had to wait till comparatively recent times — only two thousand years ago — to learn of God's wonderful vision for us? I suggest that the human race needed a process of growth in consciousness, to reach a certain point of evolution, before it was sufficiently advanced to be able to comprehend and respond to the revelation Jesus made to us.

I propose that there are four major periods in this growth of consciousness. I have written at more length about these elsewhere[1]. I call them:

1. The period of the Jewish People. The Old Testament period.
2. The period of Jesus and his disciples.
3. The period of Kingdom-Church identity.
4. The period of world Christianity, leading to the Age of the Spirit.

In graphic form the division into these periods might look like this:

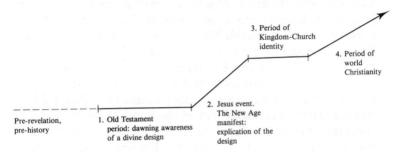

3. Period of Kingdom-Church identity

4. Period of world Christianity

2. Jesus event. The New Age manifest: explication of the design

Pre-revelation, pre-history

1. Old Testament period: dawning awareness of a divine design

1. **The period of the Jewish people** covered some 2,000 years before the birth of Jesus, during which time God formed the Israelites into a tribe which considered itself as God's Chosen People. Walbert Bühlmann has written an enlightening book, *The Chosen Peoples*, in which he makes the point that all tribes and peoples, the world over, have considered themselves to be favoured in a special way by the Supreme Deity as against all neighbouring tribes. But in our Jewish-Christian tradition we believe that it was particularly through the Jewish people that God began to make his design for humanity known.

2. **The period of Jesus and his disciples:** quite the shortest but by far the most important. During his short life Jesus achieved three things which are of such gigantic consequence that they caused the whole of humanity to take a great evolutionary leap forward. First, there was his announcement by action and word, in terms of the Kingdom, that God had a plan, a vision, a design for humanity and that with his own coming that promised new age was manifested. Secondly, by his life, death and rising to a new form of human life he empowered the whole of humankind to make the necessary breakthrough from our present powerlessness and assume the power

1. Smith, A. B. Chapters 7 and 9.

of daughters and sons of God to live a life in awareness of and governed by an entirely new God-humanity relationship. And thirdly, he gathered round him a group of people, a small community, which was to be a living declaration of this new style of life and relationships which he was inaugurating: to be proclaimed by their own manner of life and by the explanation they gave of the values by which they lived.

3. **The period of Kingdom-Church identity** reached from the time of the Apostles until our own century, covering some 1,900 years. Very soon after the death of the members of the community which Jesus formed, newly converted groups of Christians spread in all directions, but most notably Westward, into the heart of the Roman Empire. Departing from Palestine they soon broke with the synagogue. They embraced Gentile members, and with their geographical reach and numerical growth began to show all the signs of an institutionalised religion, a third force (besides Jews and pagans) to be reckoned with in the Roman Empire. With the conversion to Christianity of the Roman Emperor Constantine in the 4th century — and with him, the Empire — came the birth of Christendom, whereby the whole of the then known world claimed to live by Christian values, and the Church began to exercise temporal power. The Church and the expected Kingdom became identified, to the extent that all that Jesus had said about the Kingdom was attributed to the Church. Only with the demise of Christendom, the expansion of the Church into all continents and the encounter of Christianity with other major religions, has the Church in recent decades been able to come to a new understanding of herself not as identified with the Kingdom but as 'the initial budding forth of the Kingdom'[2]. She understands herself today, at least in theory if not yet in practice, as being at the service of the Kingdom.

The Church's perennial task is to express the Good News of the Gospel in terms that are meaningful to each age. She does not propose for our belief a series of disconnected doctrines. Hers is a single, coherent message about the God-humanity relationship. The emphasis of her presentation can change from age to age and does so under the guidance of the Spirit.

While not denying the value of varying emphases during past periods of the Church's history, we are concerned here with that particular one which has increasing meaning for us in our present

---

2. Abbott, W. LG 5.

world. While the Kingdom is our focus point today for our understanding of divine revelation, our understanding of the role of the Church is to see her, in turn, as the focus of the Kingdom, for both its proclamation and its realisation.

To say the Church is the focus of Christ's redeeming presence in our time is not to say she is its sole channel. The Church is, theoretically at least, the community which gives witness to the world of what the world is destined to become because she alone is fully conscious of the world's destiny. The theologian E. Schillebeeckx expresses the Church's role in these words:

'What the Church has to offer us explicitly is already implicitly present in human life as a whole: it is the mystery of salvation. The Church reveals, proclaims and celebrates in thankfulness the deepest dimensions of that which is being fulfilled in the world... The Church is in fact the world where the world has come fully to itself....'[3]

This is an expression of the ideal. In fact there is always a tension between Kingdom and Church. The Kingdom is the symbolic expression of God's design as eventually fulfilled when the demands made by Jesus in the Gospel are met: demands which always call us to an ideal beyond ourselves. The Church, as the expression of the Kingdom in the here and now, requiring structure, hierarchy and authority in order to preach the Kingdom, also makes demands of its members: institutional demands. These latter are more immediate and less demanding than the former which are always just beyond our reach. For that reason the institutional demands can, and mostly do, too easily eclipse the Gospel demands of Jesus. Because they are more immediate they can seem more important, whereas in fact their validity lies in the extent to which they are subservient and relative to the Gospel demands. Are not the loyalties of many Christians today to doctrine, to the Church and to the person of Jesus, in that order of priority, rather than the reverse?

The Kingdom, being greater than the Church, is promoted by all people of goodwill some of whom will be inside the Church and some outside. These promoters of the Kingdom are the New People of God of our New Testament times. 'Not everyone who calls me "Lord, Lord," will enter the Kingdom of Heaven, but only those who do what any Father in heaven wants them to do' (Mt. 7: 21).

---

3. Schillebeeckx, E. p. 82.

4. **The period of World Christianity:** is the era of our own time, and its implications for our future are the very subject this present book explores.

The expression 'World Christianity' can be understood in two senses. First, it is only within the last fifteen to twenty years that for the first time the centre of balance of Christianity has moved from the northern hemisphere to the southern hemisphere.

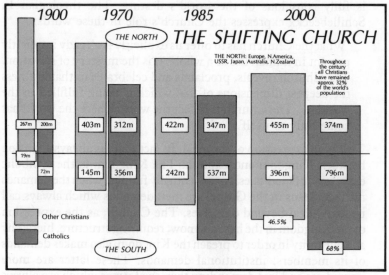

1900		**1970**		**1985**		**2000**	

THE NORTH — **THE SHIFTING CHURCH**

THE NORTH: Europe, N.America, USSR, Japan, Australia, N.Zealand

Throughout the century all Christians have remained approx. 32% of the world's population

267m	200m	403m	312m	422m	347m	455m	374m

19m

	72m	145m	356m	242m	537m	396m	796m

46.5%

Other Christians

Catholics

THE SOUTH

68%

Diagram from the Catholic Missionary Education Centre, London

Despite its claim to be catholic, the Church has until now been not simply a northern Church but very European in its theological expression, its liturgy, its Canon Law, even though it is several centuries since she expanded both East and West of Europe. Today there is no continent and hardly any country in which there is not a Christian presence even if in some countries it has temporarily gone underground. The Church is only just beginning to wake up to the implications of the shift in balance and it will be some years until we are able to boast of a Church which embraces the kind of unity which allows and grows upon diversity.

But in a second, and more profound sense, we now live in an era of 'World Christianity'. It is marked by a change of orientation from a Church which is apart from the world, pursuing her own life and drawing people into her membership for their salvation, to a Church which sees herself as part of and contributing to the totality of Creation from the inside. From a Church whose mission was to draw people in, to a Church whose mission is to go out to evangelise human culture and cultures, 'transforming humanity from within and making it new'[4].

Today we are understanding afresh that God speaks to humankind, not in abstract truths which it was the prerogative of the Church to interpret and teach, but through our culture, our history, in the great human experiences of each age: in all that goes to make up our world. That it is not in some rarified atmosphere removed from daily life that God communicates with humanity but through his own creation which in its unfolding is both the setting and the medium of his communication.

The whole world, its culture and its history, is the arena of God's saving action, that is, of his manifesting and giving growth to that Kingdom which the Church serves. 'The Church has a single intention: that God's Kingdom may come'[5].

The key to an understanding and acceptance of all the changes that have taken place in recent Church life and thinking is found in this 'paradigm shift' that has occurred: a shift from a Christianity which is Church-centred to a Christianity which is Kingdom-centred.

The term 'paradigm shift' was introduced by Thomas Kuhn in his book *The Structure of Scientific Revolutions*. From the word *paradigma*, meaning a pattern, he used it to indicate the framework or parameters within which we think about a subject. A paradigm shift means putting our thoughts on a subject into an entirely new framework.

We can illustrate this by comparing the two paradigms in the following chart which lists the characteristics of Church-orientated Christians and of Kingdom-orientated Christians. While comparing the two the reader might like to ask himself/herself with which orientation he/she feels more comfortable.

CHURCH PEOPLE	**KINGDOM PEOPLE**
Concerned with Church activities, religious behaviour, spiritual things, because these are the concerns of the Church.	Concerned with all human behaviour, everything God has made, because these are the concerns of the Gospel.
	See human affairs as saturated with spiritual meaning and Kingdom significance.

---

4. EN. Nos. 18 — 20.
5. Abbott, W. GS 45.

14

CHURCH PEOPLE	KINGDOM PEOPLE
Put Church membership above concern for justice, mercy and truth.	Seek first the Kingdom of God believing all else will follow.
Think about how to get people into the Church.	Think about how to get the Church into the world.
Their outreach is to the lapsed.	Their outreach is to everyone influential in effecting change in society.
Concerned that the Church might be changed by the world.	Work to see that the Church changes the world.
Settle for the status quo and their own (respectable) kind of people.	Are more concerned with the poor, the widow, the orphan, the marginalised.
Their Ministry is centred around Sacramental life.	Their Ministry is centred around proclamation and the means to live the Gospel values.
Hold that worship is in the first place for God's glory.	Hold that worship is in the first place for people's spiritual growth.
They can live very private religious lives.	Are concerned to build up a community as witness to the Gospel unity of humanity.
Regard those who are baptised as the New People of God.	Regard all who promote the Kingdom, baptised or not, whether Christian or not, as the New People of God.
Are concerned with the state of body and soul — principally the latter.	Are concerned with the healing and health of the whole person.

If the Good News about the Kingdom is our new pivotal point — or rather, our return to the Gospel pivotal point — we naturally want to ask what exactly Jesus meant when he spoke about the Kingdom of God. What are its characteristics, what is its essence?

Jesus himself never said, in so many words, exactly what he meant by the Kingdom. He was unable to define it both because it contains a God dimension and therefore is beyond the limitation imposed by human definition and because it is not an intellectual concept but a human experience.

We can, however, form a global idea by composing a collage of the values by which Jesus lived as expressed in his relationships with God and with people, of the explanation he gave of these values, of his proclamations about the Kingdom and of the response these brought about in the mission and teaching of his closest followers, the apostles. Perhaps the nearest we get to a biblical description we find in St. Paul's letter to the Ephesians (1:10): 'This plan, which God will complete when the time is right, is to bring all creation together, everything in heaven and on earth, with Christ as head'. Our key word might be 'unity'.

The foundation of this unity is to be the intimate relationship to which Jesus introduced us between God and human persons by expressing it in terms of a Father-child relationship, even going so far as to use the familiar child-parent term of his mother-tongue, Aramaic: 'Abba'. This approach to God was unheard of in Jewish tradition and was interpreted by the religious leaders as blasphemous. Such a child-parent relationship to God is hollow without acceptance of the consequent relationship it demands: that of relating to all people as our sisters and brothers, children of the same father. Jesus had a great deal to say about human relationships and put his word into effect by breaking down his culture's customary and conventional human barriers. From this we see that there is both a personal, interior dimension to the Kingdom — a conversion or radical re-orientation to a new way of living by a new set of moral values — and a social dimension demanding the conversion of society. We can add to this, referring back to St. Paul's 'definition' of God's design, a cosmic dimension, requiring us to live in harmony with our environment, with the totality of creation.

A Paul of our own times, Pope Paul VI, spoke of the Kingdom as the new world, 'the new state of things, the new manner of being, of living, of living in community, which the Gospel inaugurates'[6].

If, with Paul VI we can accept that 'the Kingdom is absolute and makes everything else relative'[7] because it is the human expression of God's design for his whole creation, we can better understand how it expresses the fulfilment of each person's deepest human desire to grow, to be more (fig. 1). This can be achieved by everyone only in a perfect society. The Kingdom is the expression of this perfect society, but not of a society of material values.

If we understand the Kingdom as the fulfilment of God's design for the whole of creation we can appreciate how the totality of human

---

6. EN. No. 23.
7. EN. No. 8.

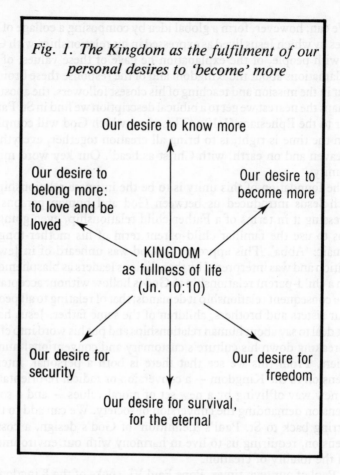

Fig. 1. *The Kingdom as the fulfilment of our personal desires to 'become' more*

Our desire to know more

Our desire to belong more: to love and be loved

Our desire to become more

KINGDOM as fullness of life (Jn. 10:10)

Our desire for security

Our desire for freedom

Our desire for survival, for the eternal

life contributes to its realisation (fig. 2). Kingdom life is not primarily religious but human. Christianity offers one possible interpretation of the Kingdom of God and, some would argue, not the best[8].

Since the Kingdom's concern is totality, unity, we can also understand how it is the centre point at which all intellectual disciplines and scientific exploration converge, no matter what be their starting point. They meet at and relate through this centre (fig. 3).

Similarly our Christian beliefs, expressed as separate doctrines, also assume a coherence when understood vis-a-vis the Kingdom as the axle of relationships (fig. 4). In this perspective, the doctrines about heaven and hell are not simply information to satisfy our curiosity about a world beyond our own, but they are to tell us something about

---

8. Sheehan, T. p. 222.

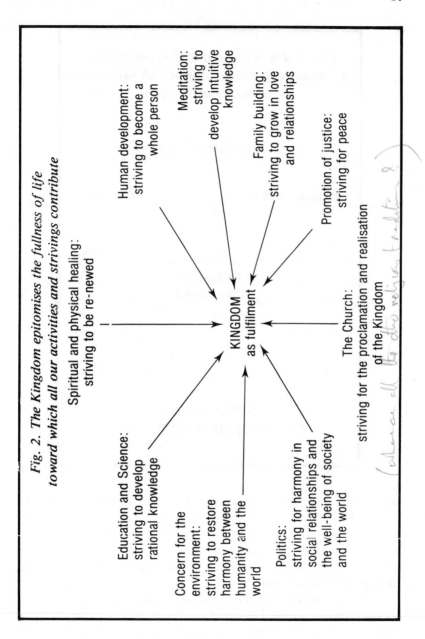

*Fig. 2. The Kingdom epitomises the fullness of life
toward which all our activities and strivings contribute*

18

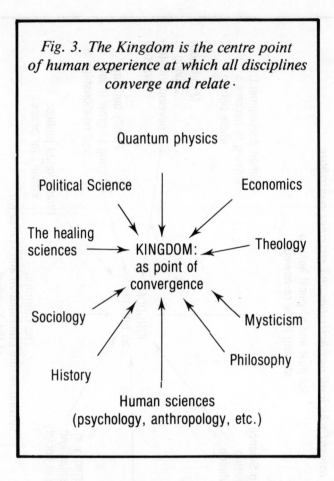

Fig. 3. The Kingdom is the centre point of human experience at which all disciplines converge and relate·

Quantum physics

Political Science

Economics

The healing sciences → KINGDOM: as point of convergence ← Theology

Sociology

Mysticism

History

Philosophy

Human sciences
(psychology, anthropology, etc.)

what we are as human persons now and of our infinite human possibilities, those to which we are orientated and those from which we are being saved. They are the two ultimate possibilities of human life, which present us already now with the two possibilities that face us daily: either openness to God's saving word or closing ourselves to it, preferring isolation.

Thus understanding the Kingdom as the summary of God's design for his creation, initiated at the beginning of time and continuing in its growth and accomplishment until the end of time, but made explicit for us in the short period of our history encountered in the pages of Scripture, we have a measure, a norm, against which we can interpet our history in its God perspective. With this yardstick we can now undertake a theological reading of the signs of the times.

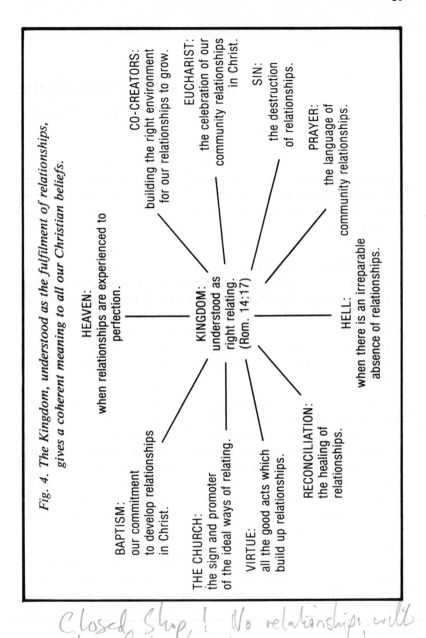

Fig. 4. The Kingdom, understood as the fulfilment of relationships,
gives a coherent meaning to all our Christian beliefs.

3. Reading the signs of the times

The expression 'the signs of the times' is used colloquially today to refer to the special characteristics of our age. We speak of the rise of unemployment or the rise in the cost of living or the increase in violence as signs of the times. The theological use of this phrase goes back to Jesus' own days. In Matthew's Gospel we read that:

'Some Pharisees and Sadducees who came to Jesus wanted to trap him, so they asked him to perform a miracle for them, to show that God approved of him. But Jesus answered, 'When the sun is setting, you say, "We are going to have fine weather, because the sky is red". And early in the morning you say, "It is going to rain, because the sky is red and dark." You can predict the weather by looking at the sky, but you cannot interpret the signs of the times!' (Matt. 16: 1–3)

Here it has quite a special meaning. The bulk of Jesus' followers were the poor, the peasants of Galilee. They were the most open to his radical message because they had nothing to lose. Here was a man with a message of hope. In his eyes they counted, they were valued, they meant something to the God he kept referring to as his and their Father. They had all to gain by accepting the new values for life that he not only proposed to them but proved were a possibility by living by them himself. Those who were most threatened by his message were those with power. They felt their authority was at risk. To accept him would spell ruin; their very status in society was being underminded. Such were the Pharisees and the Sadducees. The role of the Pharisees, a sect in Jewish society, was to further the knowledge and practice of the Law of Moses and to apply it to the circumstances of their own day. The Sadducees were a priestly party who controlled the Temple and Jewish worship. They belonged to the aristocratic upper level of society and were conservative in their views.

To the minds of both groups this revolutionary Galilean prophet must be exposed as a charlatan. And yet there must have been an element of truth in his words which resonated deeply within them. They needed to be quite sure of themselves before exposing him. They must surely have witnessed some of his previous miracles, all of which were 'signs' to those with open minds. St. John at the end of his report of the first miracle he recounts — the turning of water into wine at the wedding of friends — says 'Jesus performed this first *sign* in Cana of Galilee'. And St. Luke, reporting on Jesus' triumphant entry into Jerusalem amid the palm-waving crowds, at the end of his three years' ministry, says that the large crowd praised him 'for all the *signs* that they had seen'.

What the Pharisees and Sadducees required was obviously some physical sign that could leave them in no possible doubt. From the reply Jesus gave we might guess they asked for a sign in the sky. Maybe the sort of sign that the prophet Joel had foretold:

> 'I will give warnings on that day in the sky and on the earth; there will be bloodshed, fire and clouds of smoke.
>
> The sun will be darkened and the moon will turn red as blood before the great and terrible day of the Lord comes' (Joel 2: 30–31)

But Jesus never ever exerted that kind of mental pressure on anyone to accept his message. To have done so would have removed their freedom of choice in accepting him as the Messiah. His reply was that signs abound for those who are open enough to see and interpret them: to interpret the signs of the times. The signs of God's action in their midst.

So we notice two elements here: the sign itself and the interpretation of that sign. A sign is a symbol. It points to something beyond itself. Unless it is interpreted it has no significance as a sign. The first time I visited the small African country of Malawi, in the 1960's, there was only one set of traffic lights in the whole country, and that was to regulate traffic crossing a very narrow bridge in the centre of one of the towns. For the peasants coming into town from the rural villages they were a thing of beauty, constantly changing colour. But that was all they were. They were signs only to those who could interpret the message conveyed by the changing colours.

In the whole history of God's dealings with humankind, as related in the Old and New Testaments, we notice that God communicates himself through actions. These actions require interpretation before they become a meaningful communication, what, in theological language, we call God's Revelation.

Within our Jewish-Christian tradition we can trace the path of humanity's growth in its knowledge of God through the process of, first the Jews and later the Christians, reflecting on God's actions in relation to themselves and then, with the aid of enlightenment by the Spirit of God, interpreting these actions as signs of God's presence with his people and of the direction in which he was leading them.

The first of the historical events in this process to be recorded was the call of the patriarch Abraham to go to a new country and begin to form God's special tribe. The interpretation of these events occurred only very much later. It was while the new tribe of Israelites was wandering in the desert, having been liberated against all odds from their slavery to the Pharaohs in Egypt, that they reflected upon the evident signs of God's powerful presence among them, and understood how, step by step, they were being led by God to a special destiny. They were reading the signs of the times: the signs of God's frequent saving interventions in their history.

Right up to the end of Jesus' life on earth the small group of his disciples had still not understood the significance of who he was or the purpose of his mission. St. Luke reports that just before his Ascension they asked Jesus: 'Lord, will you at this time give the Kingdom back to Israel?' (Acts 1: 6). It was only after their enlightenment by the Spirit at Pentecost that the young community of Jesus' followers was able to reflect on the Christ-event and interpret the meaning for the whole of humanity of the incarnation, life, death and resurrection of Jesus.

It is therefore life as we experience it today that we must examine in order to understand God and the destiny which he has designed for us. This is what we mean by a theological reading of the signs of the times. 'Theological', because we are not reading the events and trends of our age as would an economist or a politician, but with the eyes of faith, confronting the signs with God's communication of himself as interpreted in the pages of Scripture, in order to read them in a God perspective.[1]

This is not a task for the individual in isolation but is the task of the Christian community as a whole: the continuing task of the Church.[2]

There are three steps in this process of discernment:

1. To observe the great movements or significant events of the time.
2. To identify trends. To understand the movements and events at a deeper than superficial level, to discover the values and human aspirations they represent.
3. To interpret them with the eyes of Faith, measuring them

---

1. 'The Church has always had the duty of scrutinising the signs of the times and of interpreting them in the light of the Gospel' (Abbott, W. GS. 4).
2. Abbott, W. GS. 44.

against the revelation of God's design for humanity which, in the last chapter, we have summarised in terms of his Kingdom.

These signs, when interpreted in this way, are never simply to satisfy an intellectual curiosity. They are a call in Faith for our free response to proclaim and commit ourselves to promote those which we discern are furthering God's overall design for humanity and at the same time they challenge us to denounce and oppose those trends in society that are militating against that design: what theologically we call the signs of sinfulness.

We are now in a position to do this exercise.

We identify trends by noting, first of all, the significant events and phenomena of our day, let us say, over the last few years. By significant, we mean not isolated events, as for example, this or that localised disaster, but those that have repercussions on a grand scale. Such would be, in recent times, the Chernobyl nuclear disaster. Although mercifully a one-off event, it had world-wide repercussions, not only in terms of human and environmental damage, but it called into question the desirability of nuclear power and emphasised the magnitude of this power vis-a-vis our human ability to control it. Such events and phenomena have to be listed at the time the exercise is done, and on every occasion the list will be different. It can help if the items on the list are classified, as for example, under the headings of:

> political
> social and cultural
> economic
> religious.

From this list we can begin to identify trends in society. By 'trends' we mean those phenomena which are not one-off occasions but movements within humanity: movements which are on the increase; the particular tides which appear to be sweeping humanity forwards in a certain direction, whether creatively or destructively.

In our present decade we can recognise the following. We identify them without making any moral judgement about them.

— the growing emergence of environmentalists and Green movements.
— the widespread experiments in genetic engineering,
— the increasing influence on public opinion by the media,
— the change in patterns of family life,
— the world-wide concern for population control, vis-a-vis world

food production and distribution,
— the rise of international organisations such as UN, OAU, EEC,
` — an increasingly wholistic[3] approach to all levels of healing, physical and spiritual,
— a greater freedom from customs, taboos and ethical parameters as humanity feels more in control of its destiny and less controlled by the powers of nature,
— a growing desire in all elements of the community for participation in decision making: a decreasing willingness to be controlled by the powerful few,
— a greater reliance on computers,
— a steady rise in the tourist industry and access to travel by more and more people,
— so many countries becoming increasingly multi-racial,
— a growing interdependence of nations: a greater sense of our belonging to one earth,
— an increasing awareness of the need for equality of the sexes,
— the probes further and further into outer space,
— the swing to right-wing conservative leadership in both politics and religion.

The purpose of this present exercise is to illustrate the process, not to supply an exhaustive list. The above are simply a few examples of the trends of our times.

Our particular concern at this point in the book is to identify what I call 'Key Trends' which, when measured against God's revelation of himself and our destiny in terms of the Kingdom, are able to give us some indication of the way humanity appears to be travelling and is likely to travel in the future. Are there indeed such trends? I believe there are. I identify four Key Trends which can be expressed in the broadest terms, and I will take each in turn and justify my choice by showing how each is really a summary of many other trends. They are:

1. An increasing humanisation
2. A global movement towards unity
3. The emergence of a new age of consciousness
4. A new understanding of God.

The figure below puts the process I have described in diagramatic form.

---

3. The word 'wholistic', (sometimes spelt 'holistic'), from the Greek *holos*, meaning 'whole', is increasingly used to describe the way in which all the diverse elements of a subject are integrated to give one all-encompassing approach. The word 'holy', coming from the same root, describes a person who is fully integrated according to God's design for us.

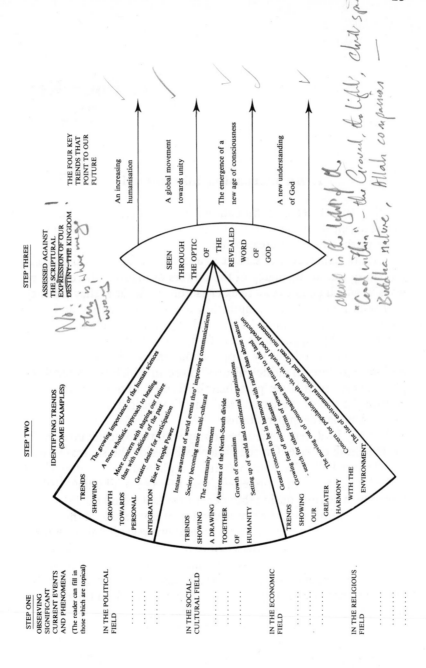

4. Four Key Trends

1. An increasing humanisation

By this title I refer to humanity's new understanding of itself as at the centre of the world. Human beings are taking the centre-stage in the drama of created life.

Until the emergence of science as a formative factor of human life, humanity was at the mercy of the powers of nature. There are two ways in which people react to external forces. As far as they can they deal with them by the strength they are able to generate and with the tools they have available. To deal with forces that exceed those capabilities they appeal to forces of a higher world to deal with them on their behalf, and this by supplications and sacrifices. We usually designate as 'pre-scientific cultures' those in which the latter force plays a very much larger part than the former. In our own scientific culture the use of the latter 'tool' has disappeared almost entirely, except among the superstitious.

As a boy I was sent sometimes to stay with two spinster great aunts in their little cottage. On the windowsill beside the staircase was a small silver bell. The aunts carefully explained to me, after I had picked it up and rung it one day, that this was a Thunder Bell. It was only to be rung during thunder storms to ward off the lightning. Today we simply run a lightning conductor up the side of the house.

In pre-scientific times the world around was regarded as potentially hostile and its unknown forces had to be appeased. Today, allowing for such exceptions as the weather and natural forces of immense magnitude—earthquakes, volcanoes, floods,—we are able to control our environment, turning deserts into fertile land and harnessing electrical, water and wind power for our use.

This has given rise to a great confidence in human ability. We feel we have become controllers of our situation.

In turn, this has led to an increasing secularisation. By this is meant not the denial of the divine in human life—we call that secularism—but a decrease in our dependence on spiritual powers, on God, to keep intervening to change the laws of nature which he has established, to meet our particular needs from moment to moment. It is often said in this regard that humanity has 'come of age.' We have passed from the dependence of childhood to a state of adult responsibility. In other words we have become more fully human by developing our latent God-given human powers.

At the same time there has been a development of the human sciences: anthropology, sociology, psychology, psychiatry. We know more about why we are as we are, both in our personal behaviour and in the way we relate to other people and to our surroundings. It gives us a freedom to challenge previous notions, beliefs and codes of behaviour. We are less enslaved by the influences of our past and can be more concerned about shaping our future, which we now feel we have the power to do.

One expression of this is the present desire felt by individuals to have a say in moulding their own and their children's future. A characteristic of our age is the desire for greater participation. We are less and less willing to allow not only natural and historical forces but also our fellow human beings to manipulate us. This is manifest in the desire for democracy, in the power of Trade Unions and, more recently, in what has been termed 'people power' by which the ordinary citizens have banded together to overthrow despotic rulers. It is seen in the power of a persecuted majority—or even minority—to obtain equal rights. It is manifest in the present world-wide campaign for equality in the rights of women. When Amnesty International was born in 1961 it was greeted as 'one of the larger lunacies of our time'. How could ordinary people, by writing polite letters to governments and dictators save the lives of people they had never met? Today, with nearly three quarters of a million members in over 150 countries it has adopted 30,000 cases of political internment. All these examples are the fruits of a greater consciousness of our human worth.

Alarm is sometimes expressed in ecclesiastical circles that this promotion of humanity means a demotion of the divine or spiritual element in life. This is the point where we have to confront this present trend in society with Scripture in order to make a judgement as to whether this secularisation is compatible with God's design for humanity, as expressed in the Kingdom, or whether it militates against it.

Does the modern cult of self-realisation and the search for the fulfiment of all our human possibilities run counter to the spirit of the Gospel? The key to our answer is found in the fact of the Incarnation: the appearance two thousand years ago of God in our midst in the human person of Jesus.

As long ago as the second century after Christ, Irenaeus wrote:

'Our Lord Jesus Christ did through his transcendent love become what we are, that we might become what he is'. And two centuries later this was echoed by Athanasius: 'He was made man that we might be made God'.

By the very fact of the Incarnation the divide between the secular and the sacred, the natural and the supernatural has been bridged. The secular has become sacred. Through the humanity of the Christ there is no area of human life which is not touched by the divine. God came into our human condition as Jesus, not to separate the spiritual from the material but to open the whole of humanity to the divine potential. Jesus as the first and only completely fulfilled human person was able to perform acts of extraordinary power—healing the crippled, raising the dead, calming the storm, walking on water—not because he drew on divine powers inaccessible to us humans but because of his human perfection. He was so perfectly evolved humanly that he was able to exercise powers which God wishes all fulfilled humanity to develop. They were not supernatural powers, they were fully developed natural powers, albeit unknown to most of us as yet. Occasionally one hears of an individual in whom this or that 'extra-ordinary' power has been developed—even if it is only that of bending spoons, detecting oil deposits by studying a map with a pendulum, producing mass hypnosis, levitating or mind-reading. The possession of such a power is no indication of the quality of that person's religious life; it is the cultivation of a power accessible by virtue of their humanity.

When we consider that through Jesus the whole of humankind is raised to a higher order of life and that he himself said that he had come 'so that you may have life—life in all its fullness' (Jn. 10:10) we can understand why St. Irenaeus could say 'The glory of God is the glory of man fully alive'. That was centuries ago. In our own time Pope Paul VI devoted an encyclical letter to the subject of human development in which he promoted the development of all people and the whole person. 'Full humanisation in unity' was how he described humanity's salvation. He went on: 'Self-fulfilment is not something optional. Human fulfilment constitutes, as it were, a summary of our duties. By reason of his union with Christ, the source of life, man attains to new fulfilment of himself, to a transcendent humanism which gives him his greatest possible perfection: this is the highest goal of personal development.'[1]

This trend to become more fully human is surely an expression of God's design for us. It is a fruit of the Incarnation, bridging the

---

1. *Populorum progressio.* N.16.

gap between the secular and the sacred, between the natural and the supernatural: causing us to become more whole.

2. A global movement towards unity

Let us recall the most helpful description we can find in Scripture to indicate the essence of the Kingdom of God as the expression of our human destiny. We find it in St. Paul's letter to the Christians in Ephesus.

'In all his wisdom and insight, God did what he had purposed, and made known to us the secret plan he had already decided to complete by means of Christ. This plan, which God will complete when the time is right, is to bring all creation together, everything in heaven and on earth, with Christ as head.' (1:8–10)

Further in the same letter he describes this in more particular terms which have relevance to his readers who as Gentiles were struggling with this new vision of humanity which had emerged from Jewish roots. Having assured them: 'You Gentiles are not foreigners or strangers any longer, you are now fellow-citizens with God's people and members of the family of God' (2: 19) and 'In union with him (Christ) you too are being built together with all the others into a place where God lives through his Spirit' (2: 22), he then spells out in more detail what this 'secret plan' is.

'In past times mankind was not told this secret, but God has revealed it now by the Spirit to his holy apostles and prophets. The secret is that by means of the Gospel the Gentiles have a part with the Jews in God's blessing: they are members of the same body and share in the promise that God made through Christ Jesus.' (3: 5–6)

In a Jewish world-view in which all humanity was divided religiously between Jews and Gentiles, Paul is saying that in the Christ era the whole of humankind has the same right to the new life in Christ. Election to special favour is no longer the prerogative of just one chosen race. *In our time election to favour is no longer the prerogative of the Church which is 'just one' religious vehicle.*

If we are able to recognise trends in world society today which are indicative of greater unity then we can interpret them as saying something to us about God accomplishing his design among us. Elsewhere[2] I have drawn up a list of many of these signs and have

2. Smith, A.B. pp. 89–93.

done so under three headings, corresponding to the goal of the Kingdom of God which is personal, social and cosmic unity:

— personal: signs of growth towards personal integration
— social: signs of the drawing together of humankind
— cosmic: signs of humanity's greater harmony with the environment.

I have already instanced some such signs in the last chapter. I will let the reader draw up his or her own list. But signs there are aplenty once we are mentally attuned to observing them: an exercise that is sometimes referred to as 'Kingdom-spotting'.

But at the same time we must have the honesty to admit that one could draw up a list of equal length of trends which show movements towards division and disunity, which militate against God's design for the unity of creation. Since the United Nations was established in 1945, to end wears and conflicts between nations once and for all, there have been 150 major wars. On the African continent alone, since the time most countries gained their independence in the sixties there have been over twenty 'wars', some continuing over most of the twenty years. But it is precisely in contrast to the varied acts of disunity and disharmony that the unity-building trends are highlighted though less acknowledged by the mass media. It is too easy to view the unit-disunity conflict as something taking place only 'out there' on the world stage and forget that we ourselves are the protagonists. The world's struggle is being battled out within the depth of each of us. It is simply another dimension of the same struggle, as the great psychologist, Carl Jung, reminds us: 'the upheaval in our world and the upheaval in consciousness are one and the same thing'. Only the arrival of the fullness of the Kingdom will see universal, inner and outer harmony. Such harmony will mark the end of time.

In the meantime there is a great polarising of good and evil taking place, and the viciousness of concentrated evil in our own day is the death-struggle of a disappearing value system faced with the emergence of a new stage in the process towards harmony.

Historians point out that civilisations go through a four-stage process of rise, growth, breakdown and disintegration. In *A Study of History*, Arnold Toynbee writes that an essential element of the breakdown is a lack of flexibility. As a defence against change, which is seen to be destructive of the pertaining social system and behaviour patterns, a civilisation becomes increasingly rigid. It is a last-ditch stand against the inevitable creative process of cultural evolution. This pattern can be seen occuring in the great civilisations of the last five thousand years: Egyptian, Syrian, Hellenic, Roman, Islamic, and more recently, Christian and Western. The social symptoms are always the same: a sense of alienation, an increase in mental illness, violent crime, social disruption. Fritjof Capra[3] adds to this list an increased interest in religious cultism. He says that the loss of flexibility causes a general loss of harmony which leads to an outbreak of social discord and disruption.

'It is evident, beyond question and beyond doubt, for all who are not entirely blind to the signs of the times, that our planet is today undergoing an acute evolutionary crisis. To the peoples of our divided world, the choice would seem to be clear—to change our ways and unite together, or to perish like the civilisations of the past.'[4]

What we must notice about the trends which point to a progress of unity among us, is not the length of the list, but the scale of their occurance. Never before has humankind thought in such global terms. We are all much more conscious these days that there is nothing that happens in any one part of our planet earth but that it has repercussions on all parts. A coup in one country, a national drought in another, the exodus of thousands of refugees in a third, is the concern of us all. Our economics are so inter-linked that a rise or fall in the price of oil, for instance, in one country affects the world market of a whole host of commodities. The increasing divide between the Northern and Southern Hemispheres is going to dictate a change in lifestyle for all people in all corners of the world before this century is out.

Never in the two or more million years of human presence on this planet has humankind been so conscious of its global responsibility. The Charter of the United Nations is a charter for every one of the five billion people now living on planet earth. It spells out the deepest aspirations of every single human being. In fact this Charter has been called the Gospel of the Twentieth Century in that through the expression of these highest human aspirations God is speaking to us today of his Will for humanity. It makes explicit humanity's longing for a World Community of justice and peace. And this too is God's design for us.

Perhaps we had a glimpse of this human desire being expressed in the mid-'80s with the overwhelming response to 'Live Aid' and 'Sport Aid' when 30 million people in 272 cities across 78 countries

3. Capra, F. pp. 7, 8, 466.
4. Brooke, A.

were involved in one great expression of solidarity with millions of their starving brothers and sisters in Africa. A further 1,500 million people in 160 countries were spectator participants through television. Perhaps for the first time on planet earth we witnessed the potential of the power of goodwill as a mass force.

Roberto Assagioli, the founder of Psychosynthesis, writes in his book, *The Act of Will*, of the wide gap between humanity's outer and inner powers. Only the development and expression of the inner qualities of compassion, a sense of justice and spiritual will, can 'offset the dangers inherent in man's losing control of the tremendous natural forces at his disposal and becoming the victim of his own achievements'.

There is one particular aspect of the current trend of unity-building which calls for special mention. It is frequently referred to as 'networking' and it happens at the local as well as at the planetary level.

Locally, it is expressed in the world-wide phenomena of basic or neighbourhood communities. The remarkable fact about the community movement is that it is a phenomenon that is found on every continent. 'Community' is a difficult word to define because it is used at one end of the spectrum by groups who associate occasionally to further some common, often idealistic, objective, but, at the other, by groups whose members reside together and hold all things in common. There is always a common interest binding them together and it can be task-orientated (to care for the mentally handicapped) or growth-orientated (a community of enclosed nuns).

Even within the limits of the Christian Church, this phenomena of 'small communities' has appeared world-wide, not as a response to a directive from above, but to answer a felt need of Christians at local level. The very spontaneity of their appearance in a variety of cultures and for an equal variety of reasons prompts one to believe that they must be the fruit of the Spirit. It is easy to understand that in Latin America such communities have been formed when people have felt the need for corporate action in order to liberate themselves from the poverty and oppression that deprives them of their dignity as persons. And one can see how, on the African Continent, an appreciation of the values of the Gospel can liberate people from a form of communal life with an interdependence based largely on a need for security and protection from exterior dangers, to a life of community freely chosen as individuals, which in turn empowers them to undertake common tasks in order to improve the quality of their lives. But what is it that is attracting the Western, self-sufficient, materially secure, often individualistic Christian towards a Basic Christian Community? It is reckoned that there are at present over 250 such Christian groups in Britain. Incidentally, well over half designate themselves as 'ecumenical' or 'inter-denominational'. What seems to be the underlying attraction towards such groups, as is also the case within those parishes which are growing into 'Communions of Neighbourhood Christian Communities', is the felt need to belong to a group in which one can relate to others at a deeper than usual level, where the members can share together their deepest spiritual experiences and aspirations, those which give meaning, give soul, to the exterior practice of their faith. Are they not filling a vacuum left by the disappearance in Western culture of the extended family?

On the wider horizon than the local situation there is appearing what seems to be a twentieth century version of ancient tribal or kinship practice. Networking—whether of individuals or of groups— has been called the antidote to alienation and is greatly fostered by present-day instantaneous world-wide communication.[5] It is the new form of institution yet differs from past institutions in that it is unstructured and ever open to change. Because it facilitates communication between like-minded people, it is not only supportive and enriching for these people but on account of the co-operation it engenders it is a powerful force for creating a new society. As we shall see later, it is the networking of individuals and groups that are concerned to usher in the new age of consciousness, that is largely responsible for this phenomenon becoming a reality, and bringing about a social transformation. The psychologist Abraham Maslow described a group he thought of as 'Transcenders', individuals whose lives were marked by frequent 'peak experiences.' He said they were irresistibly drawn to each other. Two or three would find each other in a roomful of a hundred and they were as likely to be businessmen, engineers and politicians as poets and priests. This is quoted by Marilyn Ferguson who sums up this subject by saying: 'Power is changing hands, from dying hierarchies to living networks'.[6]

This trend towards unity fulfills God's design for the whole of creation. It carriers us towards the unity of the Trinity.

3. The emergence of a New Age of consciousness

One form of networking in particular which is encompassing the entire globe is that which connects the millions of people who are aware

5. Lipnack & Stamps.
6. Ferguson, M. p. 234.

that a new human era is dawning; recognising it as an age of deeper consciousness. The phenomenon is usually referred to as 'The New Age' and its positive promotion (or, it would be more precise to say, the willed harmony which brings about a transforming power) as 'The New Age Movement'.

Today in every major city in the Western world can be found a New Age bookshop specialising in a wide variety of esoteric and human development publications and large bookshops have their section of New Age books. A variety of magazines on the subject are published quarterly or monthly: *New Humanity, Time for Living, Resurgence, Interchange, Soluna, Trans Group News, Link-up, Kindred Spirit*, to mention just a few published in Britain. In the United States they proliferate!

The wide interest this subject is generating is evident from the fact that several books which offer an explanation of the phenomenon have become 'best sellers'. The subject covers a vast field precisely because its concerns are with all aspects of life and all disciplines of study: it is a unifying movement. Here we can do no more than identify some manifestations of the phenomenon as one of our four Key Trends.[7]

There are a number of recurring themes in New Age writing and discussion which we can list as characteristics of the phenomenon:
1. That there will be a great bursting forth of human potential, physical, intellectual and spiritual: a developing of resources we hardly knew we had.
2. That the universe is shot through with living intelligence. That the whole earth is one living system, (given the name *Gaia* after the ancient Greek goddess, 'Earth Mother') which has a self-regulating ability to provide the constant and optimum conditions for the survival and development of life on this planet.[8] That humanity is part of this single system.
3. That being part of it, we have to be in harmony with, rather than to use, and abuse, creation. We are not the owners of but partners with nature. Hence the increasing ecological awareness.
4. That the consciousness of human beings is tapping into the global consciousness of our planet, bringing about a spiritual awakening

---

7. For further reading on the subject I would strongly recommend the following 'best sellers':
   The Third Wave by Alvin Toffler, (the author of *Future Shock*).
   The Turning Point by Fritjof Capra.
   The Aquarian Conspiracy by Marilyn Ferguson.
   The Awakening Earth by Peter Russell.
8. Lovelock, J.

and a raising of our level of awareness to cosmic consciousness. It is with this last that we are particularly concerned here.

Evidence of these characteristics can be found among the trends of our present society that we listed in Chapter Three (see the diagram). One aspect of these is the growing sense among people that as human beings we are not living as an isolated species. There is a unity of all on this planet formed by our drawing from a common life source. Not only are we humans united by this, but we are all participants in the source of all life, human, animal and plant. The growing awareness of this is manifested in the campaign against blood sports, the complaints about factory farming and battery hens, the outcry against vivisection, the movement for animal welfare. Of the increasing number of people becoming vegetarians today for different reasons, (an increase of one million people in Britain during 1988) a high percentage choose this diet because they find the eating of once living flesh abhorrent.

As with any new movement, the new consciousness does not just begin with a bang on a given date but develops from small seeds, from the ideas of a few isolated thinkers. Names which come to mind are: Pierre Teilhard de Chardin, C.G. Jung, Abraham Maslow, Carl Rogers and Aldous Huxley. Nevertheless such a paradigm shift as this is not simply the next step in a process of invention or education, like moving up to a higher grade in school. It is a qualitatively new way of understanding. It is not just an adding on to the old, but the taking of a step in a new direction. This is to take a risk because it means letting go of the former paradigm. Kuhn, the creator of the phrase 'paradigm shift' says: 'The transfer of allegiance from paradigm to paradigm is a conversion experience that cannot be forced'. One cannot operate from two paradigms at the same time. Two people of the past who took this risk were Copernicus in the 16th Century and later Galileo. To shift from a paradigm in which the earth was the centre of the universe to that of a sun-centred universe—and accept all the consequences—was a shift indeed and they were rewarded with the mockery and wrath of those who could not accept the shift. The writings of Copernicus were placed on the papal index of forbidden books and Galileo was hauled before the Inquisition and forced to 'abjure, curse and detest' his absurd views. These shifts are not born of more knowledge but of a new way of knowing. They burst forth from a sudden intuition.

Many authors attribute the new consciousness to an increase in intuitive (as opposed to rational) thinking[9]. And this in turn they

9. Dictionaries define 'intuition' as 'the quick perception of truth or knowledge without conscious attention or reasoning', 'knowledge from within'.

attribute to a shift from predominently left-brain thinking to an increase in right-brain thinking.

The brain has a left and a right hemisphere. The left hemisphere analyses, discriminates, measures, names and organises. Its thinking is lineal going from A to B to C, from cause to effect. The right hemisphere sees in wholes, synthesises, unites, detects patterns, comprehends the totality of A to Z. It is the creative, imaginative, non-rational part of the mind. The former is said to predominate in the masculine mind and the latter in the feminine.[10]

Our Western culture has, since the sixteenth and seventeenth centuries, favoured rational knowledge over intuitive wisdom, science over religion, competition over co-operation, always enforced by our masculine deminated society. Today, we note, there is a move to redress the imbalance, not by letting the pendulum swing the other way but by the cultivation of the whole brain. This is coming about by more people taking up the practice of deep meditation and other exercises to deepen consciousness, and also by a deliberate education policy to cultivate the creative, unifying, non-competitive potential of children. Teachers and parents remark to me that today's small children seem to be much more 'aware', 'connected' than they themselves were at that age.

Among adults too there are signs of a rapid increase of the number of people with a wholistic view of life. A facinating study of social change in the United Kingdom over the last few years[11] divides the population into three main groups: Sustenance Driven people who are motivated by the need for security and cling to an existing lifestyle, Outer Directed people who are motivated by a search for esteem and status and the Inner Directed who are motivated by self-actualization, preferring quality of life to quantity of possessions. The three types are illustrated by the reasons they would give for eating less:

The Sustenance Driven: "because food is so expensive"
The Outer Directed: "because I want to look good in my bikini"
The Inner Directed: "because I feel better for it".

The third group was hardly noticeable 25 years ago. Today they form one third of the population and are foreseen to be increasing rapidly while the other two groups are diminishing. The same pattern is found in other European countries and in North America. This is the group which is most concerned with social and ecological issues, causes

10. Russell, P. p. 191. Campbell, P. p. 44.
11. MacNulty, K

health-food shops to boom, believes that change comes about in society through a growing individual awareness and has a tendency to hold spiritual values while shunning organised, conventional religion.

Many writers within the Church[12] are recognising this emergence of a New Age of consciousness as a dynamic force. Just as there is no way to stop our exploration of outer space now that it has been set in motion, so there is no way now of holding back humankind's exploration of inner space. This was foreseen by the Jesuit paleontologist Pierre Teilhard de Chardin in the 1940s. While the word 'biosphere' is used to denote the inter-relationship of all living things on our planet, Teilhard coined the word 'noosphere' (from the Greek *noos*, 'mind') to refer to the interconnection of all human minds right round the globe and their cumulative effect. He pictured the earth as enwrapped in a human, reflective, planetary layer of consciousness daily becoming more and more complete.

If this seems far-fetched, let us look at two facts with which we are familiar. The first is the tendency of human groupings to grow ever larger. Human beings, of their nature, have always lived and worked in co-operation and not in isolation. The scattered groups of 'hunters' of the Ancient World became, some fifteen thousand years ago, settled agricultural groups establishing larger centres of social life. From villages grew larger groupings, towns, only seven or eight thousand years ago. Then came the first civilisations covering a large part of a continent. As these absorbed each other, empires were created. Today empires are giving way to global life: the awareness of our interdependence as forming one humanity on one planet.

A second fact is the growth of the collective memory and information bank of the human race. While the faculty of memory develops within each human being it is also contributing towards and able to tap a collective human memory. The traditions of our past and of each culture are stored and transmitted in language, educational systems, libraries, museums, codes of law, religious traditions, schools of philosophy and theories of science. Previously they have been geographically located. Today through the global networking of computers this great human memory bank is becoming available to any individual.

In 1988 the European Community agreed to put up half the £12m initial cost of a project to be handled by a 26-strong consortium of companies, universities and broadcasting organisations, to provide a continent-wide 'ring main' carrying voice and data traffic by early next century. The key to this new generation of technology will be

---

12. Merton, Thomas. p. 68. Happold, F.C. p. 18. Verney, Bishop Stephen. p. 13. Spink, Canon Peter. p. 14.

a tiny handset, combining telephone, television and fax machine, available to anyone at an expected cost of £40 at today's prices.

Already forty years ago Teilhard named two phenomena as contributing to the growing global consciousness. The first was the *phenomenon of unemployment.* He showed how life has always developed 'by releasing psychic forces through the medium of the mechanisms it has devised' and points to 'the growing number of people able to use their brains because they are freed from the need to labour with their hands'. He goes on: 'The attempt to suppress unemployment by incorporating the unemployed in the machine would be against the purpose of Nature and a biological absurdity. The Noosphere can function only by releasing more and more spiritual energy with an ever higher potential'. He named as a second characteristic of the present age which is contributing to the development of universal consciousness, the *phenomenon of research.* 'Research, which until yesterday was a luxury pursuit, is in process of becoming a major, indeed the principal, function of humanity.'[13] Today, tens of millions of people are employed in some form of research.

Teilhard saw the relational development of the human mind as a further step in the evolution of the human species. He referred to the fulfilment of this process, the end point towards which we are converging, as the 'Omega Point'.

A contemporary of Teihard's, a Cambridge-educated Indian mystic, Sri Aurobindo, invented the term 'Supermind' for what he believed was the next stage of evolution from matter to life to consciousness. It is to be so far beyond consciousness that it is the ultimate evolution of 'Spirit', but it will come about through the increasing spiritual growth of individual consciousness.

Scientists too are recognising after three centuries of mechanistic science that consciousness is a legitimate area of scientific enquiry. The view that consciousness is a cause of phenomena and not an effect has been advanced recently by the neuro-physiologist Sir John Eccles, the quantum physicist David Bohm and the biologist Rupert Sheldrake.

What indications are there that this New Age of Consciousness is coming to fruition now in our own times? I believe there are two: one mathematical and the other astrological.

Peter Russell[14] develops the interesting comparison, made four decades earlier by Julian Huxley,[15] between the growth of the cells

13. Teilhard de Chardin, P.
14. Russell, P. p. 77.
15. Huxley, J.

in a human brain and the quantitative growth of human brains in the world as 'cells' of a global brain, a Brain of brains. The human brain in the womb develops in two stages. Eight weeks after conception the number of nerve cells in the brain increase by many millions each day. After five weeks this process slows down. Then follows the second stage during which billions of isolated nerve cells begin making connections with each other. By the time of birth a nerve cell may communicate directly with several thousand or even as many as a quarter of a million other cells.

The average human brain contains some 100 billion[16] nerve cells (neurons) of which 10 billion are in the cortex, the area associated with conscious thought processes. Brains with only 1 billion or fewer nerve cells, such as the brain of a dog, do not have the ability of self-reflective consciousness. Only a brain the size of a human cortex allows the exercise of this faculty.

Our present planet is now populated by 5 billion brains. The increase is occuring in ever shorter intervals of time.
It took from the appearance of the first human
being until 1830 to reach 1 billion.

From 1830 to 1930 to reach 2 billion: 100 years
From 1930 to 1960 to reach 3 billion: 30 years
From 1960 to 1975 to reach 4 billion: 15 years
From 1975 to 1986 to reach 5 billion: 11 years

The UN estimates that the world population will stabilise at 10 billion in the year 2080. Ten billion is the critical figure for a new level of evolution to emerge. There are this number of atoms in a single living cell and this number of cells in the cortex of the human brain. However, Russell believes that we will not have to wait another hundred years because 5 billion is already well within the necessary range. So the first stage is complete.

The second stage depends on the intercommunication between the nerve cells—or, on the global scale, between human brains. With the fantastic speed of increase in communications it is foreseen that with the present rate of overall data processing capacity doubling every two and a half years, by the year 2000 AD the global telecommunications network could equal the complexity of the human brain. It should be noted however that this calculation is based only on the external means of communication. In the next chapter we will be saying something about the 'morphic resonance' built up by increasingly more people developing higher states of consciousness and the effects this has on other people and on the environment.

---

16. I am using the word 'billion' in its more common international usage of a thousand million.

The other indication that the New Age of Consciousness is coming to fruition in our time, comes from the field of astrology. This accounts for the fact that the emerging New Age is often referred to as the Age of Aquarius. Reference in this context to the signs of the Zodiac is not so esoteric as it might seem. Who is the reader who has not, at least occasionally, looked at the newspaper to see what advice or warning their 'sign' is offering them for that day! Besides, if we believe that the whole universe is shot through with living intelligence, it is logical to accept that the forces that maintain the galaxies affect life on this planet, and to endeavour to interpret these influences.

Astrologers divide the earth's complete orbit of the sun—one year of 365¼ days—into twelve segments each with its own zodiacal sign. Astrologers usually take the Spring (Vernal) equinox, March 21st, to be the beginning of the astrological year. So we have in turn the Vernal equinox (Aries, Taurus, Gemini), the Summer solstice (Cancer, Leo, Virgo), the Autumnal equinox (Libra, Scorpio, Sagittarius) and the Winter solstice (Capricorn, Aquarius, Pisces). What is less well known is that the whole of our solar system, of which our planet Earth is a part, moves through the heavens in a gigantic orbit of 26,000 years. This vast period of time is known in India as 'A day in the life of Brahman (God)'. Astrologers divide this great cycle too into twelve sections, each of 2,100 years during which our planet moves *backwards* through the signs of the zodiac. Jewish astrologers of Old Testament times, according to the Rabbinical writer Abarbanel, believed that the Messiah would appear in Israel when there was a conjunction of the planets Saturn and Jupiter in the constellation of Pisces. Today astronomers in their planetaria can turn the stellar clock back to reproduce the sky as it was on any day, month or year. They have discovered that there was such a conjunction in December BC 7. (Is this the explanation of the star of Bethlehem?) This provides us with a marker for the beginning of the Age of Pisces.

In a fascinating booklet, *'God and the New Age'*, the Rev. Dr. Kenneth Cuming shows how many indications there are in the Bible to this and previous ages. For two thousand years before Abraham, the Age of Taurus, the winged bull, this animal was the object of worship in Egyptian religious culture in the Minoan and Cretan civilisations and in Assyria. When Abraham was inspired to leave Ur of the Chaldees, about 2,000 BC he was moving not only from one land to another but from the worship of the winged bull to initiate the next great age, that of Aries the Ram. It was a ram that he sacrificed in place of his son and the Paschal Lamb had a great significance for his descendents from the Exodus onwards. It was not any more the object of worship but the symbol of sacrifice. Are we to understand the erecting of the Golden Calf in the widerness not only as an act of idolatry but as an attempt to thwart God's design for his people by turning the clock back to a previous age? Right up to the time of Christ the ritual slaughter of rams and lambs continued to be a central act of daily Temple worship.

The birth of the Christ ushered in the next great age, that of Pisces the fish. We cannot help but notice how prominent the fish was in New Testament times. Apart from 28 passages in the Gospels referring to fish and the promise of Jesus that the apostles were to become 'fishers of men', the fish became the great Christian symbol of the early Church appearing first in Alexandria around the year 200. The letters of the Greek word for fish, *ichthus*, was ingeniously seen to be the initial letters of the Greek words: 'Jesus Christ, Son of God, Saviour'.

And now we are another 2,000 years on, entering the Age of Aquarius whose symbol is a man pouring out a pitcher of water. Is this the age of the outpouring of the Spirit of Creativity? We are reminded of the words of the prophet Joel:

'I shall pour out my spirit on everyone:
Your sons and daughters will proclaim my message;
your old men will dream dreams,
and your young men will see visions.
At that time I will pour out my spirit even on servants, both men
and women' (2: 28–29).

During the Age of Aries, from Abraham to Christ, God as the Almighty one was predominant. During the next 2,000 years God has been manifest in Jesus the Christ. Are we now, at the turn of the millennium, entering the Age of the Spirit, a period in which humankind's relationship to God will be expressed less through the outward observance of religion, which 'The Way' of Jesus has become, but more in an inner encounter through a deeper consciousness? Astrologers characterise the Age of Aquarius as one of harmony, high moral idealism and spiritual growth. Can we pin a date to the time of transition?

The general consensus is that it was initiated in the mid 1960s. That was certainly a period when we witnessed a new outlook on life for many people: the period of the hippies, of 'flower power', the Beatles singing 'All you need is Love' and groups promoting love and peace. It was the time when seventeen states in Africa declared their independence, when the number of members in the United Nations rose to 114 (from less than half that number the previous decade), when the first man landed on the moon and Edgar Mitchell returned to say 'Each man comes back with a feeling he is no longer an American citizen—he is a planetary citizen'. It was also the period of the Second Vatican Council which opened so many windows for the Catholic Church and other Christians. This decade ushered in not a counter-culture or a reaction (which would have retained the old paradigm) but a quite new emerging culture, a new paradigm. It was not a time of religious revivial but of a transformation in consciousness.

The emergence of new consciousness—this particular Key Trend—I would suggest is a manifestation of the manner in which God, in his design for humanity, is leading us deeper into the Truth: a process unfolding in time. At the end of his life Jesus said to his closest followers:—

'The Helper will come—the Spirit who reveals the truth about God and who comes from the Father. I will send him to you from the Father, and he will speak about me' (Jn. 15:26).

Let us turn now to the fourth Key Trend and see how the Spirit is revealing 'the truth about God'.

4. A new understanding of God

It may seem strange that I list a religious subject among the four Key Trends that I believe point to the future direction humanity will take, at least in the Western world. This is not simply because our investigation is in a Christian context. It is because in every human life there is a spiritual area, consciously recognised or unconsciously present which is revealed by the manner in which a person conceives of 'God', however that ultimate reality is named, and related to. We cannot know God as God. We can only know God as diluted by our human condition. Speaking as a scientist, Heisenberg, known for his 'uncertainty principle', has said: 'What we observe is not nature, but nature exposed to our method of inquiry'.[17] If that is true about what we can know through the senses, how much more true is it of God whom we cannot observe? The God we know is a God in relation to and in terms of our humanity. Consequently ideas about God differ from culture to culture and are dependent upon our level of consciousness and on our world view. As human knowledge changes and advances into new avenues, so the human knowledge of God will change correspondingly. The world's Catholic Bishops present

17. Heisenberg, G. p. 33.

at the Second Vatican Council a generation ago acknowledged as much. In their document on 'The Church in the Modern World' they speak of the profound changes which are a characteristic of our times: 'We can speak of a true social and cultural transformation, one which has repercussions on man's religious life as well'[18]. After listing various social and psychological changes they add:

'These new conditions have their impact on religion. On the one hand a more critical ability to distinguish religion from a magical view of the world and from the superstitions which still circulate purifies religion and exacts day by day a more personal and explicit adherence to faith. As a result many persons are achieving a more vivid sense of God.'
'On the other, growing numbers of people are abandoning religion in practice'.[19]

So while some are 'achieving a more vivid sense of God' others 'are abandoning religion in practice'. In both cases there is a choice, a move from one position to another. Whether such a move is growth is a moral judgement, which we are not in a position to make about an individual.

However, just now we are not considering the individual's personal journey in his/her relationship with God—that will be for our consideration in Part Three. Here we want to see how present trends in society are pointing to the Western world's new understanding of the God-humanity relationship brought about, especially, by the increasing humanisation, about which we have already spoken, and the new cosmology, or understanding of the nature of our universe, attributable to modern science.

In examining this trend we are not saying humankind's understanding of God and expression of religious truths in the past were wrong. We are saying that they are inadequate for today's understanding of our universe.

Most of us received our religious (Christian) education based on a world view which was current until the beginning of this century:

— it thought of the world as made up of tiny building blocks of which the atom was the smallest;
— it thought of creation as something which happened once and for all a long time ago (although there were always changes, like moving the same furniture around the same room);

— it regarded the material universe as hostile to humankind and needing to be dominated for our use.

This is known as the 'classical' interpretation of our world. Continuing to operate from this world view which is no longer tenable is one of the main sources of religious controversy today and can only paralyse our capacity for spiritual growth.

To free ourselves by exploring an alternative framework—that which is multi-dimensional, wholistic, non-lineal—as a basis for our religious thinking, depends upon our being able to accept that God's Spirit is continually active in humanity leading us always onwards to a fuller understanding of Truth.

I suggest that there are four areas in which our previous understanding of God no longer fits comfortably. The first is in treating God as the supplier of our needs in the sense that he can be called upon at a moment's notice to smooth our way whether it be in providing a sunny day for our garden fete or getting us neatly through the traffic to reach the airport on time. The child in us is still comforted to think that we are able to draw on some great power 'out there', a divine parent, to order things for our benefit which are beyond our immediate control, but our adult self feels there is something inauthentic about this form of petitionary prayer. On a larger scale, our prayers to win a battle feel hollow when we know the enemy is praying for the same. So do our prayers of thanksgiving after a war when we contemplate the thousands of lives we have taken to achieve our victory. Now that we have greater power to master our world and its physical forces we are more aware of the falsity of regarding God as an instrument for our use. (What do witnesses today really believe will be the manifestation of divine power resulting from their perjury after taking an oath on the Bible in court?) With our greater scientific knowledge of the workings of our universe it feels false to continue to name God as the blanket explanation for what still remains unexplained[20].

Yet deep within us is a very human desire to call upon a source of strength beyond ourselves in moments of need. Increasingly more people are feeling that the authentic form of relating to God as the supplier of our needs is not by instant prayer as each crisis arises but through continually trying to live in greater harmony with the flow of God's creative force which orders all things.

The second area of embarrassment comes from keeping God in a separate box from life. So long as life was divided into two distinct

---

20. Davies, P. p. 209.

areas, the religious and the secular, Christians believed God could be found by withdrawing from the human and secular and entering into the 'holy' part of life. Furthermore, the religious side of life held a primacy over the secular. To turn away from the secular seems irresponsible to Christians today. They feel God must be present at the centre of their lives, where they invest most of their intellectual and emotional energies.

The third area is our inability to continue to look upon the moral life as obedience to a divine law giver. We feel uncomfortable in being chained to our childhood ideas of God-the-punisher. To bring God down to the level of our childhood understanding adults taught us that God was *hurt* or *saddened* by our sins, just as our parents were. God was presented as liking or disliking the things our parents liked or disliked, ranging from moral behaviour to table manners. Preachers maintain this attitude in adults by referring to sin as 'an offence against God', with the implication that God is 'offended' in the same way that we are when other people offend us. We will be examining our understanding of sin in a later chapter, but we can say here that the way we understand sin can throw light on how we think of God. And this in turn is revealed by our asking ourselves: am I afraid of God? It takes our growth into maturity to be able to acknowledge that forgiveness is not something God does but is our acceptance of his love.

Moral precepts used to be presented as if God had drawn up a list of arbitrary *do's* and *dont's* at the beginning of creation and that if the rules were kept ultimate salvation was assured for all people until the end of time. This may have satisfied our ancestors for whom life was simple, but today it just does not ring true. Due to technological developments the radius of personal responsibility is greater today than it has ever been in human history. We can even decide whether or not to blow up the whole human race. Our morality depends on the degree of personal responsibility to which we are summoned and this depends, in part at least, on the culture which we have created and which creates us. New moral demands are continually being made upon us, not demands which were fixed once and for all at the beginning of time, but demands which are evolving with the human world which we create for ourselves.

One author has pointed out that the Nuremburg Trials after World War II represented a moral turning point. People were no longer able to shelve moral responsibility by saying: 'I was simply obeying orders'.

Fifteen years later the world's Catholic Bishops at the Second Vatican Council were struggling with the question of the priority of personal conscience and in one of their most dramatic statement's declared that 'conscience is the most secret core and sanctuary of a man. To obey it is the very dignity of man; according to it he will be judged'[21]. The crunch was to come two years later when the theory was put into practice for millions of the world's Catholics with the publication by Pope Paul VI of the Encyclical *Humanae Vitae* on the subject of birth-control. Very soon the point at issue swung from the use of contraceptives to become an authority crisis which many saw in terms of Church authority versus personal conscience.

Exploration into the vastness of the universe and a better understanding by physicists of the nature of its origin is the cause of a fourth area of discomfort with our traditional understanding of God. To continue to believe that God created the human being as the centre and crown of all creation seems to be incompatible with our discovery that there exist galaxies and universes even further 'out there' than the galaxy M82 which is already ten million light-years from the Milky Way. Why are they there? Are they intended to serve us, and if so, how? Does life exist out there and does it need redeeming? Do they have a different 'God'? These questions, for the very vastness of their scope, will always remain unanswered.

Arguments about whether the biblical account of creation is referring to 4004 BC or 10,000 BC become irrelevant against the scientist's estimation of the earth's age as 4½ billion years and the 'big bang' of the universe as happening 12–15 billion years ago. But, more to the point, how are we to understand God's part in the creative act? To appreciate that creation is a continuous action on God's part, giving sustenance and life and growth rather than a once-for-all act billions of years ago, is one thing. But what was God's role at the beginning? We find ourselves unable to speak of God as the first cause because that presumes he existed beforehand, the first in a chain of events, but 'before' is relative to time and time is part of creation. No wonder physicists are talking about 'the self-creating universe', which is not as absurd as it seemed before we learnt how a subnuclear particle can appear from nowhere in certain high-energy processes. Paul Davies suggests[22] that God might be understood not so much as a cause of the universe as an explanation. Previously religion and science offered two rival explanations of our universe. You chose one as more satisfying and condemned the other. Today we are realising that science and religion are not in opposition but

21. Abbott, W. GS 16.
22. Davies, P. p. 45.

approach the deepest questions of existence from different starting points. Science is based on observation and experience of the physical universe, while religious knowledge comes from revelation and intuitive wisdom.

In so far as we try to handle these questions with our imagination we might be helped by borrowing a concept from Eastern cosmology and speak of God unmanifest and God manifest where the latter is the God of our limited human understanding. For the former, the Protestant theologian, Paul Tillich suggests the appelation 'the God above God'[23]. Already in the 13th century Meister Eckhart the German mystic had made the distinction between God and Godhead[24].

We are shifting from thinking of God as a supreme being 'out there' to God as the power at the centre of our being, at the centre of all being, calling and empowering us to reach beyond ourselves. Unfortunately the Church in her worship still prefers the biblical references to God as a being beyond humanity such as Creator, Lord, Almighty, rather than employing other scriptural names: Truth, Wisdom, Love and Life, which relate to the deepest dimension of our lives.

The Anglican Bishop John Robinson caused a stir in 1963 when he had the courage to publish *Honest to God* in which he grappled with these new concepts of God. Yet what he said struck a chord of authenticity in the hearts of thousands of Christians. What he dared to say then is much more widely accepted today. Gregory Baum expresses our contemporary thinking in these words:

> 'God is not an object of which man may have an observer knowledge. Why? Because God is present in the very man who knows God and in the very process of knowing God.'
> 'That God is present *in* history and hence not a being ruling history from above is at the very heart of the Christian revelation.'[25]

Elsewhere he describes God as 'the uncreated depth dimension of human life' and as 'the transcendent mystery present in history.'[26]

The recognition of 'God at the centre' is a recognition of the great change now taking place within Christianity, a change in religious consciousness. Christians are becoming less dependent on theologians and Church doctrine to tell them *about* God but are seeking a direct

---

23. Tillich, P. p. 180.
24. Weber, R. p. 168.
25. Baum, G. p. 178.
26. Baum, G. p. 189.

experience of God. They are relying less on their rational knowledge
to learn about a God outside and more on their intuitive knowledge
to experience God at the centre of their being. Direct experience is
first-hand knowledge: doctrine is second-hand knowledge.

Doctrine about God is the preserve of the believer, but intuitive
knowledge of God is available to everyone, it is part of our humanity.
Which is why we find so many expressions of the transcendent in
secular writing today: *Absolute Consciousness, Creative Intelligence,
The Grand Unifying Theory, The Unified Field, The One Supreme
Universal Power.* They are all expressions of unity, of wholeness: they
all mean God.

Is this Key Trend compatible with the unfolding of God's design?
I believe it is because each step draws humanity closer into the
Godhead.

As God's design has unfolded over the centuries in human
consciousness there has been a parallel growth in humanity's
understanding of who God is in relation to the human being. Within
the Old Testament we find a development from the notion of there
being many gods of whom the god of Abraham was one, to the god
of the tribe of Israel who was the supreme god, to a more refined
understanding that there is only one God.

The next great step in our understanding came with the arrival
of Jesus on the scene and his teaching us to have a Father-child
relationship to God.

Although this introduced a new dimension—a new intimacy—it
was not the last word. It could not be. The value of the 'Father' image
is conditioned by an individual's experience of fatherly or parental
love. Besides, it distracts from the maternal aspect of God.
Furthermore, it tends to cause us to think of God as a super-human,
thus nourishing, rather than weaning us from our child-parent
dependency.[27]

Very recently, however, an event took place which shifted us into
yet another understanding of the God-humanity relationship. In this
respect it is just as significant as the first Christmas day. And the
two dates have this in common: their significance was unnoticed at
the time. They only became remarkable dates when their consequence
became apparent.

The date I refer to is 6th August 1945: the day of the explosion
of the first Atomic Bomb. It killed 75,000 people in Hiroshima and
injured tens of thousands of others for life. It was the day that put

---

27. This shift is clearly explained in a new book by John Wijngaards: *God Within
Us.*

into the hands of humanity a power that previously belonged only to God. It was the first step along the path to our present position where we possess 20,000 megatons of nuclear explosives. (One megaton alone is equal to the explosive yield of 80 times Hiroshima.) Human beings now possess the power to destroy the whole of humanity and all other forms of life.

Before 6th August 1945 we had understood God to be the sole creator and sustainer of human life and implicit in that was the belief that he was the sole terminator of life as a whole. We have now assumed this power for ourselves. We co-create with God by allowing life to continue. We now share the mastery over the life of our world with God. God is no longer 'Almighty God'. God can no longer be understood as being externally related to the world as the power that totally controls it.

This moves us into an age in which our understanding of God has to be interiorised: from the Almighty God out there to God the dynamic, creative power within the very centre of all being: God as Spirit.

5. Two catalysts

In the world of chemistry the word 'catalyst' is used to refer to some substance added to a process in order to accelerate the chemical reaction.

As distinct from the four Key Trends that I have identified and elaborated upon in the last chapter, I observe two other trends—characteristic of our times—that are exercising considerable influence on the other four and causing them to evolve at an increasing speed. The first is a social catalyst, in that it is present in society as a whole and influences the whole of humanity without any wilful choice on our part. The second I call a personal catalyst in that it is an action of individuals and although performed by only a minority—albeit a growing minority—it is having global consequences on the development of the Four Key trends. I shall treat each in turn. They are:

1. The acceleration of change in society.
2. The increasing number of people practising some form of deep meditation.

1. The social catalyst

Since living beings are not static but always moving through cycles of birth, growth, maturity, death and, in the case of human beings, re-birth, change is a fundamental quality of all life.

Within that part of creation which is our main concern here—humanity—change has been evident since the first human beings appeared on earth. We are not speaking now of geographical change, movement from one environment to another, but of that process of change which is called development: a progress from the old to the new, where the new evolves from the old.

In Chapter Four I have already spoken of the evolution from a pre-scientific to a scientific age. (Alvin Toffler calculates that ninety per cent of all the scientists who ever lived are alive today.[1]) But change can be traced also in the manner in which human beings organise their

---

1. Sadly, half the world's scientists and technologists are employed in war research and development. (Lonergan & Richards. p. 81.)

relations with other human beings (on the cultural, political planes), in the way in which the human person relates to the world of the supernatural (on the religious plane) and (on the plane of knowledge) in the development of and self-reflection on our own consciousness.

Whether such changes are an improvement or a deterioration is a moral judgement to be made by assessing them against what we believe is the final destiny of humanity. Do they help us reach that destiny or deter us from it? At this moment I am not making such a judgement but am concerned with the phenomenon of change as such.

So what is so special about change in our own time? It is not that change continues to be a condition of human life but the speed at which change is accelerating. It is the nature of change to gather momentum. Alvin Toffler in his book about change, gives a number of illustrations of the accelerating pace of change. I will draw on just one of his illustrations—that concerning modes and speed of travel[2]—and put it in the form of a chart.

Form of transport	Average speed	From
The camel	8 mph	6,000 BC
The mail coach	10 mph	1784
The steam train	13 mph	1825
Developed steam train	100 mph	1880
Flying	400 mph	1938
Rocket plane	4,800 mph	1960s
Space capsules	18,000 mph	

In human terms, the teenager in Western society today is surrounded by twice as much of everything humanly-made as his parents were at the time he was an infant. By the time this teenager reaches 30 he will be surrounded by twice as much again. This production of goods has required a consumption of energy. Half of all the energy the human race has consumed in the past 2,000 years has been consumed in the last one hundred. Toffler calls his book *Future Shock*. Such rapid change brings about a culture shock that the human physical and mental system is quite unprepared for.

While this acceleration of change is the product of the human mind, it has at the same time overtaken the mind's ability to cope with it. Researchers into human behaviour agree on two facts: that the human mind has a limited capacity to adapt to change, and that overloading the system leads to a serious breakdown of performance at the levels of perceiving, thinking and decision-making. Accelerated

2. Toffler, A. *Future Shock*. p.33.

change is surely to blame for the breakdown of so many behaviour patterns today, ranging from our tolerance level of stress to our political and economic systems.

The days are gone when one generation would draw up the plans for a cathedral and lay the foundations, leaving it to the second and third to complete it for the benefit of generations in the following centuries. One of the great engineering feats of our day is the building of the Channel Tunnel. It has been on and off the drawing boards since my grandfather's day but now that the plan is being executed it is expected to be complete in five years, and even this seems to us to be a long time. We are very unwilling to invest in something from which we ourselves will not benefit.

The shift from a static to a dynamic, evolutionary concept of reality, a result of our experience of change, causes us to understand in a different way many passages of Scripture. For instance it was possible formerly to read the passages about creation as an event which took place once and for all in the past, and was then complete. Today such a literal interpretation has become impossible. It no longer rings true to think of God creating the earth with its plants, its animals and its human population and since that time simply keeping his creation in being (divine preservation) and ruling over human history (divine government). We now view our world as continually evolving, continually being created, and as moving towards a completion which will be worked out in a God-humanity partnership.[3]

Our present day dynamic perspective causes us to understand creation as a process, not as an event. One which, from its very beginning, is a spiritual as well as a physical process.[4] When we listen to God's summons to us to grow and become more—more fully human—we enter into the continuing process of creation. This is why many biblical scholars today re-read the Genesis account of Adam, as God's perfect creation, and of the Garden of Eden as the perfect world, not as describing a past situation but as a projection into the future, a description of the promised human destiny.

Similarly, we can no longer think of two great historical divine events separated in time—the first being creation and the second, to correct our sinfulness, redemption. God's ongoing creative act is always redemptive, is always an empowering of humanity to reach

---

3. This concept is referred to in theology as *Synergism*. The word *synergy* derives from the Greek *syn-ergos* meaning 'to work together'. In the past, Christian theology taught that God was the sole agent and would have regarded Synergism as a version of the Palagian heresy. (See Don Cupitt. *Life Lines*).

4. Lonergan & Richards. p.25.

the perfection destined for it. I will have reason to say more about 'redemption', understood as an empowering for growth, in Part Two.

Our previous static concept of reality caused us to look backwards, regarding Creation, the Fall, Redemption as divine actions in the past. Our present dynamic perspective forces us to see them as present realities, always in the 'now'. We are being caused to look forwards, to accept our responsibility for creating our future.

Human beings, alone of all creation, are privileged to change the manner of ordering their lives according to their wishes. A bee lives out its destiny in a very complex social system from which it cannot break out. It has operated the same system for thousands of years and will continue to do so until it becomes extinct. Only we human beings are able to cause our pattern of life to change, to shape our destiny. But the speed of change has now acquired a dynamic of its own which has outgrown our control.

2. The personal catalyst

Under this heading I am referring to the fact of and the effect of an increasing number of people practising some form of deep meditation.

By 'deep meditation' I refer to that technique which enables the mind to settle down so that it is in contact with the centre of our being. It is the way to pass beyond the senses, beyond the rational mind, to experience something of the transcendent reality. As such it is simply a human activity. For religious people, this entry into the transcendental is a prayer, a non-conceptual prayer rooted in the silence of the heart.

In traditional Western spirituality we use the word 'meditation' to refer to that discursive method of prayer whereby we take a passage of Scripture or other writing and, with our rational mind, ponder it and apply it to our personal spiritual life. We use the word 'contemplation' to speak of the exercise of our intuitive mind, whereby we open ourselves to the work of the Spirit within us in what we might describe as a state of active-passivity. Apart from disposing ourselves to the Spirit's action, we are not mentally active, but simply alert. In traditional Eastern spirituality the two words 'meditation' and 'contemplation' are used with exactly reversed meaning. I make this point because many of the methods or techniques of meditation that are increasingly in use in the West today come to us from the East. This is why I am using the term here 'deep meditation' to mean what Western Christians would refer to as contemplation: the exercise of the intuitive mind.

Among such methods are different forms of Yoga, Zen, Sufism, the hypnotic chanting of mantras and a variety of techniques offered by different schools of meditation: Silva Mind Control, Est, Transcendental Meditation. What they all have in common is to provide a means for the mind to rise to a higher state of consciousness.

Higher than what? Human beings normally exercise three states of consciousness and apart from exceptional moments, pass the whole of life in these three. They are the state of deep sleep when the body and the conscious mind are fully at rest, so deeply in fact that we are unaware that we are in this state at the time and only realise we have been in it when we wake from it. Secondly, there is the twilight state, the dream state, when the body is at rest and the mind is relaxed and not under conscious control, but when we are aware of all sorts of disconnected thoughts passing through the mind. It usually precedes or follows deep sleep. The third is the wakeful, alert state in which we spend most of our day, when both body and mind are active and influencing each other. Higher than these most authors describe four further states which go by various names and are less clearly defined, for instance, transcendental consciousness (or pure awareness), cosmic consciousness, God consciousness and Unity consciousness.[5] The great Western mystics, for example St. Theresa of Avila and St. John of the Cross, have their own way of describing these states or mansions of the mind in terms which are more poetic and symbolic than scientific. But the details of these need not concern us here. The point I am making is that increasingly more people are employing one or other technique to transcend the three lower states of human experience, and so enter a higher than normal state.

There is a variety of reasons why people set out on this journey. Broadly speaking, they fall into two categories. There are those who do so for what we might call physical or mental reasons. They are promised by their instructor that such a practice leads to greater harmony of body and mind and will cause such benefits as a lowering of blood pressure, loss of weight, a feeling of well-being, a cure for cancer, greater sensitivity in human relationships, an improved memory, etc. Then there are those who do so for spiritual reasons: for a deeper form of (contemplative) prayer, an awakening of their religious faith, a new consciousness of 'the truth as it is in Jesus' (Eph. 4:21).

The effect of this practice is wholistic, to bring body and mind into harmony. Therefore those of the first category soon discover

5. For a clear description of these states see Anthony Campbell's *Seven States of Consciousness*.

that the spiritual side of their life is also being awakened while those of the second find that their new spiritual exercise is benefiting their general well-being and their social relationships too. In a word, deep meditation induces greater harmony in all areas of human life.

But why am I proposing that the phenomenon of increasingly more people taking up this practice should have, as one effect, an acceleration of the four Key Trends we have identified? Because the new age of which they are indicative is not primarily an age of new social concern or of global politics or of more just economies but a new age of conciousness. The exaggeration of our left-brain, rational approach to life's problems which has dominated the Western world's thought processes for so many centuries, is now being balanced by the cultivation of more right-brain intuitive thinking. And the practice of deep meditation is one of the main contributory factors.

But is this practice becoming so wide-spread as to have a world-wide influence? I can speak only of one such technique from personal experience and shall draw my examples from that: Transcendental Meditation as taught by Maharishi Mahesh Yogi, and commonly referred to as 'TM'. The movement currently claims that some three and a half million people have been taught this technique world-wide since the 1950s when Maharishi first introduced it to the Western world under the title of 'The Spiritual Regeneration Movement'.[6]

To what extent are the effects of TM measurable? The physical effects on the individual meditating—the changes in the EEG (electro-encephalogram) patterns indicating the relaxation of the nervous system, the slower rate of heart-beat (as indicated by a drop in the rate and volume of breathing) and the fall in the metabolic rate (the rate at which the body burns up its fuel) can all be measured scientifically by repeated controlled tests. The effect upon the environment however, can be measured only circumstantially rather than scientifically and therefore with less accuracy. Such environmental effects as the lowering of the level of stress and its consequences can be observed in areas where 1% of the population is practising TM. These are, for instance, a decrease in the crime rate, a drop in the number of hospital admissions, a fall in the number of accidents, less violence. There is no way of knowing whether these measurable effects are due simply to the percentage of people of a given area practising TM, as the TM organisation would claim, or whether they are the consequences of the number of people practising

---

6. The Movement claims that of these three and a half million meditators some 55,000 have been taught the advanced TM-Sidhi programme which has a much more powerful environmental effect. In Great Britain the figures are 150,000 and 2,000 respectively.

regular deep meditation in a variety of ways, including, for instance, the presence in the area of a monastery of contemplative monks or nuns. But whatever the form the practice takes, what connection is there between the exercise of this small minority and the observable facts?

The theory that explains this connection goes by a variety of names: Morphic Resonance, the Morphogenetic Field, Formative Causation, and in the case of the TM movement, the Maharishi Effect.[7] The theory is that when only a small percentage of people make a breakthrough in consciousness this empowers vastly more people to make the same breakthrough. There is a reported instance of this in the animal kingdom that has become a classic example. A biologist, Lyall Watson, tells of the behaviour of a monkey tribe on an island off Japan.[8] Researchers, studying their feeding habits, had given them a supply of sweet potatoes. The freshly dug potatoes were covered with dirt and the monkeys were not tempted by them. One day a young monkey dipped her potato in the sea before eating it. The cleaner potato and the salty taste made it much more appetising. She did the same next day and the following days. One by one the other monkeys began to copy her behaviour. Gradually the habit spread from moneky to monkey until it became a universal practice. Watson goes on:

'Let us say, for argument's sake, that the number (of potato washers) was 99 and that at 11 o'clock on a Tuesday morning, one further convert was added to the fold in the usual way. But the addition of the hundredth monkey apparently carried the number across some sort of threshold, pushing it through a kind of critical mass, because by that evening almost everyone in the colony was doing it. Not only that, but the habit seems to have jumped natural barriers and to have appeared spontaneously...in colonies on other islands and on the mainland in a troop at Takasakiyama.'

Nearer home, we could postulate that one day a blue tit discovered that if it pierced the top of a milk bottle with its beak it had access to an appetising drink. No blue tit schools gave lessons in this technique, yet we now find these birds doing the same thing all over the country.

On the human level, do we not notice that children today learn to ride a bicycle almost spontaneously whereas we acquired the art only after many a spill? Even allowing that 'cycles today are of an

---

7. For a fuller description refer to Aron, E & A.
8. Watson, L. *Lifetide.* p.157.

improved design, can we not say that the art seems to be so widely transmitted that it has become an automatic part of our human mechanism? Are we today witnessing a generation picking up a facility for computer programming in the same way?

People practising deep meditation as a group often find that their meditation experience is more profound than when they meditate alone. Furthermore, experiments have revealed that when a large group of people were meditating together—in this case TM—a smaller group a thousand miles away experienced an increased coherence between the individuals while they meditated, even though they did not know at what time the larger group was meditating. That is, the pattern of brain activity of the second group was more in tune with each other than usual. Peter Russell[9] recounts this experiment and goes on to suggest that during meditation people are setting up resonating electromagnetic waves around the planet.

Dr. Rupert Sheldrake, a biochemist, has built up a new theory—that of 'Formative Causation'—of how life evolves, from experiments in the plant and animal kingdoms in which he has observed the same effects. For instance when a collection of rats has learned a new pattern of behaviour, other rats, all over the world, tend to learn the same pattern more easily.

In the Autumn of 1984 he conducted an experiment on the 'Tomorrow's World' programme of BBC TV. A member of the audience was asked to choose between two pictures made up of blotches. To most people the image in the picture was impossible to identify, (Fig. 1). The selected picture was then shown to viewers and the image revealed. So there were now two pictures: one incomprehensible and the other revealed to an estimated 8 million viewers. In the following weeks the two blob pictures were shown to six thousand people in Britain and 12 other countries who had not seen the TV programme. In continental Europe 33% of people shown the picture that had been revealed to viewers were able to recognise it while there was no significant change in the small percentage able to recognise the second blob picture.

The fact of the transmission over a distance of thought, consciousness, energy, even evil, is not new to us. We call it telepathy. In the Middle Ages in Europe and still in Africa today, evil can be wished upon an absent person by sticking pins in a doll . . . and the results are remarkable! The Church has always expressed the effects of an individual's good or evil actions upon other people in terms of our being one body in Christ. The effects of the historic event of the

---

9. Russell, P. pp. 172–173.

This is the hidden-image picture that was shown.

death and resurrection of Jesus upon the whole of humanity has been explained for centuries in terms of 'grace'. We shall be suggesting in Part Two that this explanation of *how* the effect of one man's action can influence the lives of all people of all time is less than satisfying in our own day.

Today we are understanding these influences in terms of global consciousness. What we notice is that numbers seem to play an important part. Watson writing about the monkeys suggests that 100 is a significant number. Maharishi has claimed that if 1% of the population were practising TM the course of history would be profoundly altered.[10] George Gurdjieff, the Russian mystic and teacher said that just 100 fully enlightened people would be sufficient to change the world.

10. Through many years of scientific research the Maharishi International University (in Iowa, USA) has found that the formula required to create coherence in the collective consciousness of a given population is for the square root of one per cent of that population to be practising the TM-Sidhi programme. Maharishi is currently trying to gather together in one place a permanent group of 7,000 such meditators. 7,000 is the square root of one per cent of the world's present population.

Even in the Old Testament (Gen. 18: 23–32) we find an illustration of the spiritual influence of the few upon the many. We are told of Abraham pleading with the Lord to spare the city of Sodom from destruction if only a handful of just men can be found among the guilty inhabitants. After a lot of bargaining by Abraham, the Lord promises to spare the city if there are found as few as ten just men.

An analysis of statistics for crime rate has been made of 22 cities in the USA, with a population over 25,000 and comparable regarding income, education, unemployment, age, etc. In 11 over 1% of the population had been taught TM whereas the other 11 had considerably less than 1%. During the control period (1972–73), in the non–1% the crime rate increased by 8.3% in line with the national average, whereas in the 1% meditating cities it actually *decreased* by 8.2%.[11]

If the effect of thousands of people meditating is to be a significant catalyst for the whole planet, its effect must be seen to have an influence wider than on a few isolated cities. Lately it has been found to have international effect. I will give just one example from the many available. It concerns Zambia when I was living there, in the late 1970s. It was the time of the Rhodesian Unilateral Declaration of Independence and guerilla fighters were being trained in their thousands in neighbouring Zambia. On account of the worsening relations between the two countries Maharishi sent some twenty meditators (practising the advanced TM-Sidhi programme which has not a 1% but an estimated 1 to a 1,000 effect), to Zambia and forty to Rhodesia. In Rhodesia the average daily deaths due to the civil war were 27 in the early days of November 1978. During the period the meditators were there, from 5th—27th the average went down to 4 a day (though, curiously, rising to 11 when the meditators split into two groups of twenty, one group in Salisbury and the other 300 miles away in Bulawayo, in order to spread their influence—which seems to prove the value of concentrating the effect). The daily deaths rose again to 28 per day when they left on November 28th. Four days before the arrival of the Zambian group, Rhodesia bombed Zambia's capital, Lusaka, and anti-white feeling ran high in the city. During the meditating period not only was calm restored but even the economy, depending 90% on the mining industry, picked up. There was a decrease in the violence and the terrorist gang was caught. The day after the meditators left (December 22nd) there was another Rhodesian bombing raid on Zambia. A coincidence? It could be said to be. But similar instances have been documented in Rhode

---

11. Statistics from Aron, E & A.

60

Island (USA), Nicaragua, Iran, Israel and South East Asia, and in the early 80's in Holland, Puerto Rico and Delhi.

During 1986 a body based in Texas called the Planetary Commission for Global Healing attempted to reach 'the critical mass of human consciousness' by enlisting 500 million people in 77 countries to spend an hour in 'healing meditation' at 12 noon local time on December 31st 1986 so that there would be a 24 hour period of meditation being done by 10% of the world's population. The number reached 800 million in 1987. During 1988 we saw peace 'breaking-out' in more places than we have seen in previous decades. Another coincidence?

Whatever doubts we might have about the validity of statistics for particular occasions we must surely agree with the views of Sir George Trevelyan:

> 'Though he is but a tiny unit in himself, man meditating is performing a deed of cosmic significance. By each meditation we align with a universal process. Man is the catalyst that can allow the redemptive events to occur, so that the Spirit can impregnate the body of earth.'[12]

The blob picture revealed.
(Pictures reproduced by permission of Dr. Rupert Sheldrake.)

---

12. Trevelyan, G. p. 151.

Part Two

Where the signs are pointing

Chapter Six states the central thought of this book. This raises questions that are studied in the following chapters. No attempt is made to *prove* points—this would require a book on each topic: others have done the spadework for that already. The purpose here is to 'make connections' and allow the reader to draw his/her own conclusions . . . and move on from there.

6. The New Age: The Age of the Spirit

I am persuaded that the 'signs of the times' that we have examined thus far point in one direction: that we stand at the breakthrough point of what is being widely described as a 'New Age', and that not by accident this corresponds with our passing from the second to the third millennium of the Christ time. This awareness is expressed in the quotation from Pope John Paul II at the front of this book.

I have already used T.S. Kuhn's expression, a paradigm shift, to emphasise that this New Age marks an evolution in consciousness, a fundamentally new way of understanding life with a consequent change in the patterns of human behaviour.

James Robertson provides a useful summary of the two paradigms:[1]

From	**To**
Scientific and academic knowledge	Intuitive understanding
Representative politics and bureaucratic government	Community politics and direct democracy
The institutional economy based on money and jobs	The gift and barter economy of households and local communities
An arm's length relationship between professionals and their clients	Personally shared experience
Institutionalised social services	Caring personal relationships
Organised religious activity and codified religious doctrines.	Personal spiritual experience

---

1. Robertson, J. pp. 66–67.

It will be noticed from Robertson's second column that the indications are that we are moving into an era in which our relationships are more fully human and therefore more in accord with the Gospel's Kingdom values.

A word of explanation needs to be added at this point about the relationship between the New Age and our biblical understanding of the Kingdom of God.

The secular use of the term 'New Age' refers to our present-day shift of paradigm as marking our own changing times and the emergence of a new consciousness. In this sense the New Age is also referred to as the 'Age of Aquarius'. Many Christian writers, however, use the expression 'New Age' to refer to an event two thousand years ago: the manifestation of the Kingdom of God by the Christ and the paradigm shift that this initiated. There is no contradiction here.

The manifestation of the Kingdom was like the appearance of the first shoots of a seed planted long before. The shift we are experiencing today is caused by the maturing of that plant and its sudden bursting out into flower. This present New Age, understood in the perspective of the Kingdom of God, is the fourth and present era of that Kingdom, the period of world Christianity.

Having said that, I am not implying that in our present paradigm shift we are about to experience the *fulfilment* of the Kingdom. What I am saying is that we are entering an Age in which humanity as a whole is going to experience what the message of Jesus is all about; an insight that till now has been the privilege of only a few.

I have explained already that the reason why Jesus the Christ did not appear on earth for some two or more million years, but came among us only two thousand years ago was that the human race needed a process of growth in consciousness before it was sufficiently advanced to be able to comprehend and accept the revelation and message Jesus brought; even to understand that the Good News of the Gospel is Good News about humanity and what humanity is called to become. The present break-through is into an era in which the Good News will become meaningful to humanity as a whole. What Jesus announced as present as a potential is about to become an actuality.

The message of the Kingdom has to be reinterpreted by each culture in each age according to the current level of consciousness. Indeed, even in reading about the original announcement of the Kingdom in any part of the New Testament we have always to ask who was the audience or readership that the preacher or writer was communicating with and what was the purpose of saying this particular thing in this particular way. Jesus' announcement of the Kingdom of God was made to the peasants of Galilee, poor people who were regarded as second-class citizens by the priestly aristocracy in Jerusalem, the Sadducees. He did not preach violence against Roman occupation as did the Zealots, but a message to build up their human self-respect; a message that is summed up in the Beatitudes. For Paul, preaching later, outside Palestine, to Christians mostly in an urban setting who were suffering as individuals, the main thrust was the cross of Christ through which salvation—an individual affair—was offered. In his letters the social dimension of the Kingdom takes second place. Today, when we are regaining our sense of community, our planetary oneness, calling for justice for all peoples and appreciating the wholeness of creation, we are interpreting the Kingdom as applying to the whole of humanity and as having cosmic significance.

This is the era in which we are understanding the implications of the Kingdom being more extensive than the Church. We are able to recognise God's action in his world outside and beyond the Church because we recognise the presence of Kingdom values in the lives of people who have different religious affiliations from our own, or none.

When we read, for example, that during 1988 more than 14 million people in Britain applied for donor cards (as against 5 million in 1987), signifying their willingness to allow their hearts, lungs, livers, kidneys and other organs to be used for transplant operations, we recognise here a concern for the quality of other peoples' lives which cannot be explained as having any religious motivation, nor by any desire for reward or fame or domination or even gratitude. It is a demonstration of the Kingdom value of altruism. The same must be said of the universal and instantaneous response to appeals to relieve the famine in Sudan and Ethiopia or to meet the human needs arising from floods in Bangladesh or the earthquake in Iran. Such increasing human concern can only arise from a growing sense of identity with our fellow human beings beyond the boundaries of culture, religion, language or race: a new universalism, a Kingdom quality.

Cultures and circumstances can change but the message of the Kingdom is universally applicable. '. . . the created things will be shaken and removed, so that the things that cannot be shaken will remain. Let us be thankful, then, because we receive a Kingdom that cannot be shaken.' (Heb 12: 27–28).

The central thought of this book is that all the 'signs of the times' are indicating that the whole of humanity today is taking a great leap forward into a New Age of consciousness that points towards the fullness of the Kingdom which was manifested by Jesus the Christ.

I am proposing that we can interpret our human history, in a

66

Christian perspective, as passing through three Ages of God-humanity relationship.
I shall call them:

> The Age of God the Almighty
> The Age of God the Familiar
> The Age of God the Spirit

Although the move from one age to the next is by a quantum leap in the consciousness of our God-humanity relationship, rather than a steady growth, it is not a question of the next age discarding the former age and completely replacing it. The new stage is the perfection of the previous one, as the grub buried in the earth moving upwards in one dimension becomes a caterpillar, limited to movement in two dimensions, then breaks through into the butterfly which can enjoy movement in three dimensions. But it is the same creature making the break-through. I have called it a leap forward in consciousness of our God-humanity relationship because it is this which determines our whole approach to religion, worship, morality and human relationships. This will become clearer as we look at the characteristics of each age in turn.

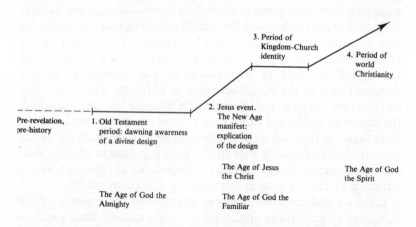

Fig. 8 superimposes the Ages on the diagram we saw in Chapter Two.

The Age of God the Almighty

This age covers the period of the two millennia before Christ, beginning where Jewish history begins, with the call of Abraham. These two thousand years are sometimes called the Age of God the

Father[2]. This appellation might cause us to think that during this period—which we call Old Testament times—God was known as Father in the same way in which we address him today. The title 'Father' is found in Old Testament writings but it is used to refer to God as the creator, the provider, the winner of battles on the Israelite's behalf, the guardian of the Jewish Tribe. It is not at all the understanding of God as the intimate Father to which Jesus was to introduce us.

Since, as I have said, each Age is not vacuum-sealed from the next but the seeds of the next are planted in the former Age, we should not be surprised to find reference in the Old Testament to God's tenderness. For example God's motherly attributes are recalled by Isaiah.

During those two thousand years as the Jewish people went through a process of refinement in their understanding of God, their deity became in their eyes a fearsome cosmic sovereign, the judge of all peoples who demanded obedience to an externally-imposed and eternally-binding law as the way to salvation. The relationship between God and the Israelites was that of King to servants. Their greatness as a people depended upon their loyalty to the Divine King of the tribe, which was expressed as a bargain between themselves and God: the Covenant. The source of their strength and their growth as a people was through their faithfulness to the Covenant. Indeed, the Covenant was their theological paradigm: it gave meaning to the their God- humanity relationship. God's presence with his people was chiefly thought of in physical terms: his presence in the Temple in Jerusalem. Their knowledge of God grew through an external revelation: reflecting upon God's action in their life as a people and interpreting this, especially through the voices of the prophets. So a development of this understanding occurred in the 5th Century BC when the Babylonian army attacked Jerusalem, destroyed the Temple of Solomon and led the King of Judah and some 10,000 of his people back to Babylon as captives: that period known in Jewish history as the Exile. There, in Babylonia, the prophet Jeremiah encouraged the captives to pray to the God whose presence they had previously limited to Palestine. From this experience grew their idea of there being only one universal God.

There was a parallel moral development, particularly from a collective to an individual morality, and a growth in their understanding of justice and forgiveness. Evil was expressed in terms

---

2. Cupitt, D. 1982. pp. 61–62.

of breaking the Covenant. It was atoned for by retribution, and by renewal of the Covenant.

The Age of God the Familiar

Then into the tribe of the Chosen People came Jesus to usher in the next two thousand year period of religious history. I have called this era the Age of God the Familiar because, although the life of Jesus was orientated to the traditional God over and above this earth, he related to God in a completely new and personal way. Jesus used the name *Abba*, an Aramaic word, which was an intimate family term, so new to Jewish ears as used of God that such familiarity with God was considered blasphemous. He taught that God's presence is to be found also within our own selves and within each other person. Our love for God is to be expressed in our loving our neighbour. Evil is expressed as personal sin: an evil committed against one's neighbour is a sin against God. While it was to be taught later by his followers that remission of sin is obtained for the whole of humanity through atonement made to God by the death of Jesus, it is gained for each individual by personally seeking forgiveness of the offended, both God and neighbour.

In the decades and centuries following the short life of Jesus his liberating message and the manner of living it became institutionalised. The living experience of the 'Good News' as seen and heard in Jesus encountered the Greek world of philosophers where it became intellectualised. As the liberal Protestant scholar, Adolf von Harnack, has said: 'When the Messiah became Logos the Gospel became theology'. After a few hundred years the Fall-Redemption became the theological paradigm into which framework the rest of theology was fitted. Salvation came through Church membership, the Church being identified with what Jesus had said about the Kingdom of God. The chief means of grace for spiritual growth was administered by the Church through Sacraments and the main thrust of evangelisation was the saving of the individual soul. The Church became the custodian of Truth, the interpreter of revelation and logically the herald of the Good News. Christianity grew to become a world religion claiming superiority over other world religions.

The above characteristics of the Religious Ages of the last four millennia are of necessity sketchy. The intention is not to offer a description of the Judeo-Christian religion but to flesh out the chart at the end of this chapter. It is the emerging Age which is of particular interest to us here and this is the subject of the rest of this book. But to help in the understanding of the chart let me continue with a resumé of what will be the traits of the Age of God the Spirit.

The Age of the Holy Spirit

Many of the characteristics of this emerging age can be identified in the four Key Trends that we studied in Part One. It is the era in which the human person 'comes of age'. Von Hugel speaks of three steps in the progression of Christianity as a religion. From the conversion of the Emperor Constantine and the birth of the Holy Roman Empire in the 4th Century until the Enlightenment in the 18th Century the Church exercised supreme authority in the Western world. This step was the age of the Institution; the age of religious childhood, of personal dependence on outside authority in the search for Truth. This was the age when theology was considered the Queen of Sciences and all phenomena were explained theologically, which in turn often meant being explained according to a literal interpretation of the Bible. The Enlightenment ushered in the supremacy of intellectual and scientific investigation: the period of religious adolescence, a pulling away from the control of the Church. This gave birth to our present stage of secularisation where we offer scientific rather than theological explanations of events not because we belittle God but because we have a more mature understanding of his creating role. It purifies religion by enabling us to disengage it from a magical view of the world.

Von Hugel sees us now taking the third step, into the mystical stage, that of adulthood.

One of the great shifts between the last and the New Age is in our understanding of God. In Chapter Four we spoke of the embarrassment of people today in accepting the traditional image of God as a Supreme Being 'out there' controlling all things. What words does one use to describe God according to the emerging understanding? Bishop Robinson offered us a description in his *Honest to God*: 'The ultimate depth of all our being, the creative ground and meaning of all our existence'.[3] The real difficulty in finding the right words is not that the words are inappropriate but that words—any words—are not helpful. In moving into the mystical era we are less concerned with saying anything at all *about* God because our concern is with an *experience* of God. At first sight the Robinson 'definition' seems to move us away from the personal 'Father God' to an 'It-God'. Our experience of God as present in the depth of our being, however, is very personal indeed.

A question favoured by surveys of the degree of religiosity of 'the person in the street' is: 'Do you believe in a personal God?' It contains an ambiguity. 'Person' is a word we use to identify a human being:

3. p. 47.

God is not a human being. (No wonder people have difficulties with the imagery evoked by the 'Three persons in one God' definition of the Trinity!) If the survey question were rephrased: 'Do you relate to God in a personal way?' the answer would be 'Yes'—if they did. The first is a static question, the second dynamic. God is not a person but our relationship to God is personal because it is a dialogue between us as persons with God who is person. When we say 'God is person' we do not mean God is *a* person, *another* person than you or me, but that in God is found to an infinite degree our highest attributes as persons: our ability to know (intelligence) and our ability to love (free will). These are the two faculties with which we are able to relate to God in dialogue. So our relationship to God in the deepest dimension of our life is personal. It is not an 'it' relationship of cause to effect (God being the cause and us the effect) but of us the recipients to God the giver, of us the listeners to God who calls us, of us the unable to God the enabler. In other words, our relationship to God is not between things or objects but it is dialogic.

Since the New Age is an age of new human consciousness it obviously implies a new way of understanding Truth. The root of the present unease which is destabilising the Church right across its spectrum, from conservatives to liberals, from evangelicals to ecumenicals, lies in the different understanding of what theology calls 'Revelation': the way in which God communicates Truth to us. It is an unease caused by the idea of a God out there communicating facts about himself, and that through simply one channel: the Church. So long as the Church's main emphasis is on the teaching of facts *about* God—external revelation—through her liturgy, her catechetics, her social action, her dogmatic statements, (all of which appeal to our rational knowledge) while neglecting to help people to encounter God directly through intuitive knowledge, the unease will grow. As people are becoming more intuitive they are shifting from concern about religious facts to a desire for religious experience; from passively accepting to be told what to believe by an external authority to individual subjectivity, from the security of conformity to a search for religious meaning which is life-giving and life-transforming. People are becoming less concerned today whether this or that article of the Creed corresponds to objective reality. What is true for people today is whatever gives meaning and worth to their lives—that is where Truth lies. Again, a swing from a static to a dynamic view of life.

One illustration of a new, more positive way of thinking is in the development by the North American Dominican, Matthew Fox, and his companions, of what they call Creation Spirituality.[4] They argue

---

4. Particularly recommended is his book: *Original Blessing*.

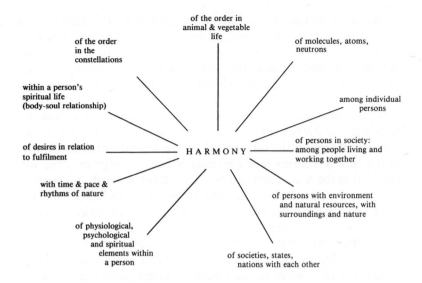

of the order in
animal & vegetable
life

of the order
in the
constellations

of molecules, atoms,
neutrons

within a person's
spiritual life
(body-soul relationship)

among individual
persons

of desires in relation
to fulfilment

HARMONY

of persons in society:
among people living and
working together

with time & pace &
rhythms of nature

of persons with environment
and natural resources, with
surroundings and nature

of physiological,
psychological
and spiritual
elements within
a person

of societies, states,
nations with each other

Fig. 9. All are aspects of the harmony within creation: an attribute of the Creator.

that Western spirituality has two basic traditions. The one with which we are all familiar starts with the experience of sin and develops a theology and spirituality based on our need of redemption (the Fall-Redemption paradigm). Hence our preoccupation with personal sinfulness and our readiness to view the world as a place of temptation and despair. The other, Creation Spirituality, starts with the experience of life—the Original Blessing of creation preceded the Original Sin—and emphasises the goodness and positiveness of creation. Fox maintains in fact that the Creation paradigm pre-dates by several centuries the Fall-Redemption paradigm.

One of the key concepts of the Age of the Spirit is 'harmony'. It is not only a recognition of the harmony in creation but a realisation that disharmony impedes the evolutionary process, while to be in harmony with it is a source of both individual and social growth. Harmony is not a passive state. It is unity in action: it is about our manner of relating. Let us put this in diagramatic form. To the intuitive mind diagrams say more than verbal descriptions!

A great deal is made today of efficiency. It is one of the most highly esteemed values in Western society. If only we could learn the value of harmony as our *idée force* to replace efficiency we would be much more efficient because harmony seeks to 'go along with' the natural creative forces.

Finally, let it be said that talk of an Age of the Spirit is not new.

In past centuries there have been groups in the Church and individual mystics who proposed that such would come. Of special note among the speculations, on account of its similarity with what is proposed here, is that of the Cistercian abbot and mystic Joachim of Flora in the 12th Century. He proposed that there were three ages of the world corresponding to the three persons of the Trinity. The first age, corresponding to the Old Testament dispensation, was that in which the Father ruled, representing power and inspiring fear. The second period he understood as that of the Christian Church of the New Testament when wisdom, hidden through the ages, was revealed in the Son. The third period he foresaw would come about after some great cataclysm in 1260. It was to be the Kingdom of the Holy Spirit, a new dispensation of universal love which was to proceed from the gospel of the Christ but transcend the letter of it and in which there would be no need for disciplinary institutions.

In 1200 Joachim submitted all his writings to Pope Innocent III but died in 1202 before any judgement had been passed. In the middle of that century a sect arose among the Franciscans, the Joachimists, to propagate his prophecy. They produced many writings which they attributed to Joachim, but in fact going far beyond what the abbot had taught. This work was condemned by Pope Alexander IV in 1256. The year 1260 came and went without incident and after that little more was heard of his prophency. But let it be added that Abbot Joachim, though never officially beatified by the Church, has ever since been venerated as a 'beatus'!

The authorities in the Church of his time quashed his notions along with those of the Joachimists because they implied a criticism of the Church. Why such a projection is different in our own day is because it is so universally recognised and so widely demonstrated by our planet's present crisis: the crisis that we have already mentioned, caused by an emerging culture challenging an existing culture and resulting in this latter raising the drawbridge and defending itself.

The emergence of the New Age of the Spirit will see—is already seeing—such a defensive action being fought at least in some quarters of the Church. The hard conservative line taken by Archbishop Lefebvre and his following after the Second Vatican Council is an extreme example. As the shift increases from a religion mediated by authorities to one of direct spiritual experience, those who seek their security in an unchanging tradition are going to feel threatened. The way in which the Church expresses her understanding of herself and gives a living witness of the Kingdom of God is going to have to change greatly, even radically, and before the turn of the century.

The big question is whether this change will result in a breakdown or a breakthrough for the Church.

Before we are in a position to attempt an answer to that question we need to give some consideration to the role of formalised religion in humanity's spiritual evolution.

EVOLUTION OF THE CHRISTIAN PARADIGM

(N.B. Items give predominant, not exclusive categories. There is an over-lapping across the Ages)

	THE AGE OF GOD THE ALMIGHTY	THE AGE OF JESUS THE CHRIST. GOD THE FAMILIAR	THE AGE OF THE HOLY SPIRIT GOD THE SPIRIT
	2 millennia BC	2 millennia AD	3rd millennium AD onwards
The word 'God' denotes	Lord, as cosmic sovereign	Person, Father-figure – out there	The ultimate depth of our being, the creative ground and meaning of all existence.
God reveals himself principally	Through external revelation, believed by the Israelites to be exclusive to them.	Through external revelation, epitomised in Jesus and believed by the Church to be exclusive to her	Through internal revelation, intuitive knowledge, open to all who seek
Understanding of God's presence with us	In the Temple in Jerusalem	In Christ present in humanity. The Mystical Body. The Temple of the Holy Spirit	In the centre of our being. The world as the Temple of God
Religion	Tribal religion	Christianity, a world-wide religion.	Transcendence of all religions
The theological paradigm	God's Covenant with a chosen people	Fall-Redemption	Creation: progressive evolving
Religious imperative	Sociological. Obedience to an externally imposed law.	Membership of the Church, the Body of Christ.	Personal growth to our full spiritual-human potential.
Central act of worship	The Temple sacrifices	Jesus' eternal sacrifice. The Eucharist as sacrifice.	The Eucharist as meal: eschatological banquet.

EVOLUTION OF THE CHRISTIAN PARADIGM (Cont'd)

(N.B. Items give predominant, not exclusive categories. There is an over-lapping across the Ages)

	THE AGE OF GOD THE ALMIGHTY	THE AGE OF JESUS THE CHRIST. GOD THE FAMILIAR	THE AGE OF THE HOLY SPIRIT GOD THE SPIRIT
Evil expressed as	Breaking the Covenant. Ritual morality	Personal or social sin: an offence — against God (analogically) — against neighbour	A blockage to one's own or another's growth. A cause of disharmony
Healing by	Atonement, retribution. Renewal of Covenant	Forgiveness by the one offended	Removal of blockage to growth
Means of spiritual growth	Faithfulness to the Law of Moses	Openness to grace, eg. through Sacraments	Transcendence through deep meditation
The Good News	In terms of being a chosen people with the promise of a Messiah	In terms of personal salvation (Heb. 9: 12)	In terms of enlightenment, new consciousness, growing harmony. (Jn. 17: 3)
Kingdom understanding	Israel is God's Kingdom	'The Kingdom of God is among you' (Lk. 17: 21)	'The Kingdom of God is within you' (Lk. 17: 21)
Love for God expressed through . . .	Faithfulness to the Covenant	Relationships — with (intimate) God — with other human beings	Harmonious relationships — within self: body and mind — self with others — self with environment
Human relationships	'Love your neighbour as you love yourself (Lev. 19: 18)	'Love one another as I have loved you' (Jn. 13: 34)	'. . . that they may be one, just as you and I are one' (Jn. 17: 22)
Heralds of the Good News	The Prophets	The Church	The New People of God
Astrological age	Aries — Ram sacrifices	Pisces — ICHTHUS = Christ	Aquarius — outpouring of the Spirit

7. The Religion Era

There are many books being published today which attempt to predict the course our planet is taking as a consequence of our leap into the New Age of consciousness. Some deal with the phenomenon from a scientific angle, others forecast the effect on world society, others again are concerned with the field of communications and computer networking, while still others try to predict our future economic patterns or the development of our sources of energy.[1] Our particular concern here is with the human-God relationship and the indications we have of how this will evolve. Since, as we have already said, we are unable to rationalise about God as Absolute, our concern is always with God as relative, relative to our human condition. God the Absolute is unchanging: the God-human relationship is always changing because the human element is in perpetual change. We may pass into periods of 'God-is-Dead' and out into 'God-is-Alive-again'. This leaves God unaffected: it is we who are changing in our current understanding.

Since life for the human being exists in time—is in progress—and since the human being has the capacity to reflect on his or her progress, a deep psychological need we all have is to give meaning to life, as Carl Jung emphasised. Without meaning human life disintegrates. We can even accept suffering when we are able to give it meaning.

It is the spiritual dimension of human life that has attempted to provide the ultimate meaning. An awareness that we are called to something greater than, something beyond ourselves. 'Religion' is the institutionalised form that our spiritual dimension takes. We cannot be non-spiritual because that is part of our condition as creatures living on a time-space earth. Our condition invites us—compels us—to relate: to relate to the beyond time and space, to relate to other human beings and to relate to all else on planet earth. The very word 'religion' comes from the Latin root *re-ligare:* to bind together.

---

1. Particularly recommended are *The Gaia Atlas of Planet Management* (Ed. Norman Myers) and *The Gaia Peace Atlas* (Ed. Frank Barnaby).

Diarmuid Ó Murchú, in his fascinating study of the human person's need for God, *The God who Becomes Redundant*, shows how the externals of religion evolved slowly in human history as did other cultural features:

+ 2,000,000BC	First human beings
600,000	Discovery of fire
150,000	Dwelling in caves
100,000	Ability to use a language
50,000	*Evidence of religious ritual, especially in burial customs*
35,000	Development of art
25,000	Use of stone 'blades'
20,000	Flute music. *Signs of explicit religion*
15,000	First houses
5,000	Script writing. Towns began to grow into cities of 10,000 inhabitants
3,600	*Temples*

It would appear that only from about 20,000 BC onwards—in the last 1% of humanity's existence on earth—are there any signs of explicit religion, the emergence of cults with a system of gods, priests, worship, sacrifice and divine and priestly kingship. Only in this period does there appear to be any speculation about the gods and their powers for good and evil in the universe.

The point that Ó Murchú goes on to make is that it is only comparatively recently that major religions began to appear, Hinduism being the first, around 2,000 BC. Formal religion comprises only about 6% of the history of the human religious story. Judaism emerged only around 1,200 BC. The centuries 600–300 BC saw a decisive step forward in human consciousness. It was the Golden Age of Greek thought (with Plato and Aristotle) and the birth of other great religions: Zoroastrianism, Taosim, Confucianism and Buddhism. (Islam, of course, followed much later, 600 AD, from the roots of Judaism.)

The late appearance of formal religions in human history causes us to ask how necessary are they to human life? Are they a phenomena of a transient stage of human evolution out of which we are now passing in our progression to a higher state of consciousness? The very idea of religions as separate communities is a comparatively modern invention. In none of the great religious scriptures is there a word which corresponds to our modern concept of 'religion' or 'religions'.

Is St. Paul's famous chapter on Love (I Cor. 13) telling us that ultimately what counts is each person's spiritual experience? Creeds and doctrine are each religion's attempt to explain the cause of and to interpret the meaning of that spiritual experience which is common, in varying degrees, to the whole of humankind. In Europe, since the Enlightenment, the search for meaning has moved from the religious to the secular and scientific. In our own time the pendulum is swinging back, but not the whole way. It is swinging back to the spiritual element of human life, but not to institutionalised religion.

Irrespective of formalised religion the human person has the capacity to transcend towards a richer, fuller sense of wholeness. God is present in the very act of creation and God's spirit is present within every human being, causing each person to be a spiritual being. (Christian baptism does not confer the Holy Spirit upon a person in whom the Spirit was previously absent. It is an act by which we acknowledge, and more important, respond to that presence.) Every human being is spiritual, but not necessarily religious. Spiritual humanity existed for some 50,000 years before religious humanity emerged (around 2,000 BC). As Ó Murchú puts it: 'Religious man is a relatively recent visitor to our planet'. And he rightly goes on to say: 'It is not appropriate to suggest that religious man is a better spiritual person than his non-religious predecessors'.[2]

It was Alister Hardy, a biologist, who proposed the hypothesis that experience of God is 'a biological fact'. In 1984 the Alister Hardy Research Centre was set up at Manchester College, Oxford, to collect, monitor and analyse accounts of religious and spiritual experiences in individuals, regardless of their religious context or affiliation, to test Hardy's hypothesis. He had previously set up a Religious Experience Research Unit in 1969, and this unit had studied more than 4,000 case histories of individuals who had had some form of religious experience. A similar research carried out at Nottingham University on a national scale with a sample of 2,000 people suggested that more than 30% of the adult population in Britain has had such an experience. The experiences recorded, drawn from people in all walks of life, include being bathed, surrounded or suffused in light, which is variously described as pure, white or brilliant, accompanying strong flashes of insight into the nature of self and the universe, or feelings of inexplicable release and joy. 'It does not appear true, as Freud would have had us believe, that religious experience is associated with mental imbalance or weakness', said Edmond Robinson, the Centre's director at the time. 'It is much more associated with psychological maturity and personal integration. Nor

---

2. 1986. pp.34–35.

is it associated, as Marx said, with the downtrodden and the oppressed, but on the whole with people who are well-adjusted, and even comfortable, in their lives.' The existing evidence is sufficiently varied for Robinson to suggest that essentially religious experience is the same, no matter from what tradition it comes.[3]

The present director, David Hay, says that when they did more detailed in-depth studies, but still on random samples of smaller groups (e.g. university students, adult members of the population of the City of Nottingham, nurses in Leeds) the positive response rate went up to over 60%, but about 40% had not told anyone else about it, not even people as close as husband and wife. They were frightened of being labelled stupid or mentally unbalanced. He adds that in both Britain and the United States, Catholics on the whole are less likely than Protestants to claim to have had this kind of experience.[4]

In 1975 the National Opinion Research Corporation in the USA reported that more than 40% of the adults polled there believed they had had a genuine mystical experience.

So, religious or mystical experience is no more connected with a religion than is salvation—and it is certainly no monopoly of Christianity. It can be experienced by people with no previous spiritual awareness, that is, awareness of the realm of the spiritual within us as different from the physical or mental. It does, however, lead to an awareness of that spiritual realm.[5] The danger lies in people interpreting such experience, as was the case in the Middle Ages, as a recognition by God of the person's sanctity or, equally dangerous, in the opposite direction, in our attributing mystical experience to some evil force or its personification, Satan.

Christianity a religion?

It will have been noticed that in the above reference to the birth of the great religions I did not mention Christianity. Today Christianity is indeed one of the world religions, in fact numerically the largest. The reason for the omission is that we need to examine whether Jesus ever intended that what he was proposing to humanity should eventually become a Religion or whether it was a new way of living which through historical events became institutionalised. This becomes a particularly relevant question when we come to consider

---

3. Reported in the Sunday Times, 14th November 1984.
4. Writing in the Catholic Herald 10th April, 1987.
5. J.M. Cohen and J.F. Phipps have collected together a vast number of such experiences in their book *The Common Experience*.

80

the future of the Church in the New Age, as we shall be doing in the next chapter.

There is much talk today about Sects and New Religious Movements, in fact the Vatican has recently conducted a worldwide research into these. They are not recent phenomena. They have been the product of all the great religions throughout their history. We can say that the Jesus movement began as such in the eyes of its contemporaries and from the sociological viewpoint the Prophet Jesus is in the same category as Muhammed, Simon Kimbangu in Zaire and Mr. Moon. The reports of one of the workshops at the 1975 Assembly of the World Council of Churches in Nairobi states quite simply: 'The Christian Gospel creates community . . . It does not create 'Christianity' as a philosophy or a system'.[6]

Jesus formed a group around him, a community of disciples, who by their way of life and their message were to continue his mission of making the Christ Age a reality. It was as simple as that. They were in fact called 'The Way' and were regarded in the period following Pentecost as yet another sub-group of Jewish life, as were the Pharisees, the Sadducees, the Essenes, the Zealots, the Qumran community. Jesus prescribed no new form of worship, so they continued with their Jewish worship, going to the Temple in Jerusalem each day for prayer (Acts 3: 1); they observed the Jewish diets (Acts 10: 14), and continued to circumcise their sons (Acts 21: 21). They did not see themselves as any different from their co-religionists except that they recognised that the promised Messiah had come, a new age had begun: they were fulfilled Jews. Their mission to make known this new way of being a Jew was articulated by the angel who released the Apostles from jail: he instructed them: 'Go and stand in the Temple, and tell the people all about this new life' (Acts 5: 20). As the Christian Jews later found themselves among Gentile people, their leaders—the Apostles—began to understand they had a mission beyond Palestine. This cultural leap out of Judaism was the birth of the Jesus-movement as a Religion.

A Religion, as an institution, has four characteristics:

1. a doctrine of beliefs, usually summed up in a Creed;
2. a moral code;
3. a way of worship, a cult;
4. an authority structure;

which together offer a way to find a fuller life, and provide a meaning for this one. Or, put another way, it is a religion's purpose to make

6. *Breaking Barriers: Nairobi 1975.* (Ed. David M. Paton). p. 74.

it known that every person is called to be united with God and to offer the means to accomplish this.[7]

Let us look at these one by one and see how they related to Jesus' actions and words.

1. *A doctrine of beliefs.* Jesus' teaching was pragmatic, not theoretical. It was all about relationships—between people and God and between people themselves—expressed in terms of the Kingdom of God. What is remarkable is that whenever faced with a speculative question he gave an illustrative, pragmatic answer. In fact most of his answers slightly side-stepped the question put. He was concerned not to let his listeners be occupied with abstract matters but to bring their minds to bear on their manner of living and relating. The supreme example was when faced with Pilate's philosophical question 'What is Truth?' He gave no reply: the question was inappropriate, and there is no answer. So he gave us no doctrinal definitions—not even of the Kingdom. He mentioned three different aspects of God: it was only much later that theologians categorised them as a Trinity. He supplied no formula of beliefs: credal statements developed later in the Church. Indeed, he never even required faith in any doctrine; only in himself as the Messiah who was ushering in a new age. 'Whoever believes in me, streams of life-giving water will pour out from his heart' (Jn. 7: 38).

The message he brought was not announced to the Rabbinical school trained in the Law of Moses, nor was it a secret teaching imparted only to a select group. He would speak to anyone who would listen. Apart from Jerusalem he appears not to have taught in any of the cities of Judea or Galilee but to have confined himself to obscure villages, to places like Nazareth and Capernaum which were obscure enough not even to have obtained a mention in the Old Testament.

His choice of followers who were to be bearers of his Good News is significant. Since he was not forming a new religion or a new institution he did not require people who could assimilate and then proclaim convincingly a new doctrine or theory, nor even those possessing organisational ability. He required disciples who were open enough to be touched by the radical nature of his message, who would be fired with enthusiasm because they had experienced in his company a new appreciation of the worth of each human person, and above all, a new way of relating to God through an intimate child-parent relationship.

---

7. Griffiths, Bede. p. 108.

He realised that their level of awareness could not absorb all that he wanted to share with them, but during his Last Supper in their company he promised that at a later time his Spirit would enlighten them—and us—still further:

"I have much more to tell you, but now it would be too much for you to bear. When, however, the Spirit comes, who reveals the truth about God, he will lead you into all the truth.' (Jn. 16: 12–13)

The Spirit in fact would enable them to 'hear' at a deeper level what they were hearing from him at a surface level. 'He (the Spirit) will give me glory because he will take what I say and tell it to you' (Jn. 16: 14).

2. *A moral code*. 'The Son of Man is master of the Sabbath' (Mt. 12: 8). 'The Sabbath was made for the good of man; man was not made for the Sabbath' (Mk. 2: 27). Jesus did not present a new, alternative moral code but raised the Jewish code to a higher level. In Chapter 5 of Matthew's Gospel six paragraphs of Jesus' Sermon on the Mount begin 'You have heard what people were told in the past, but I tell you . . .' He did not abolish the existing law; he raised it to new heights (Mt. 5: 17). He stressed the primacy of justice as the foundation for the new relationships he proposed. In this he reminded them of the Jewish prophets: 'It is kindness that I want, not animal sacrifices' (Hos. 6: 6, Mt. 12: 7). He elevated what was the basic code of behaviour of all cultures[8]: 'Do for others what you want them to do for you' (Mt. 7: 12) and replaced it with 'a new commandment': 'As I have loved you, so you must love one another' (Jn. 13: 10). He gave universal

---

8. *Zoroastrianism:* Do not do unto others all that which is not well for oneself. (Dadistan-i-Dinik)
Confucianism: What you do not want done to yourself, do not do to others.
Buddhism: Hurt not others with that which pains thyself. (Udana-Varqa)
Jainism: Refrain from inflicting upon others such injury as would appear indescribable to us if inflicted upon ourselves.
Plato: (Greek philosphy): May I do to others as I would they should do unto me.
Hinduism: Do naught to others which if done to thee would cause thee pain. (The Mahabharata)
Islam: No man is a true believer unless he desireth for his brother that which he desireth for himself. (Hadith)
Sikhism: As thou deemest thyself, so deem others. Then shalt thou become a partner in heaven.
Taoism: Regard your neighbour's gain as your own gain, and your neighbour's loss as your own loss.

application in a 'new and eternal covenant' to what had been a covenant between God and one chosen race.

3. *A way of worship, a cult.* Jesus never organised any religious service or prayer meeting, nor left any instructions for worship with his followers. He himself never called people to worship. Indeed, in Jewish terms he was a layman, not a member of the priestly class. As a good Jew he observed the Jewish festivals, he demanded respect for the Temple (Mt. 21: 12–13), and used the village synagogues to preach the arrival of the Kingdom age (Lk. 4: 44). Religious observances like fasting he put into a new perspective (Mt. 6: 16–18). Although the external Temple worship was central to his own Jewish life he foretold the time when it would be superseded by an interior spirituality: 'The time is coming and is already here, when by the power of God's Spirit people will worship the Father as he really is, offering him the true worship that he wants. God is Spirit, and only by the power of his Spirit can people worship him as he really is' (Jn. 4: 23–24). Later the disciple John in writing of the revelation given him of 'the new Jerusalem' wrote: 'I did not see a temple in the city, because its temple is the Lord God Almighty and the Lamb' (Rev. 21: 22). Jesus had already spoken of himself, as the manifestation of God, as being a greater presence of God on earth than the Temple in Jerusalem: 'I tell you that there is something here greater than the Temple' (Mt. 12: 6).

In place of instructions about worship, he told his followers that in his memory they should share a meal (I Cor. 11: 23–25): an expression of fellowship, a symbol of unity—of comm-union with himself and through him, with each other.

His very incarnation—God made manifest in human life and taking part in all our human activities—bridged the divide between the sacred and the secular, as was dramatically symbolised at the moment of his death when the curtain in the Temple, concealing the Holy of Holies, the innermost sanctuary, 'was torn in two from top to bottom' (Mt. 27: 51). As the author of the letter to the Hebrews expresses it: 'We have, then, my brothers, complete freedom to go into the Holy of Holies by means of the death of Jesus. He opened for us a new way, a living way, through the curtain—that is, through his own body' (10: 19–20).

4. *An authority structure.* The only form of authority structure Jesus proposed was that Peter should be the leader of his group of followers. We might imagine that had he lived longer and had more time to organise his mission he might have left behind a more structured community, as has been the case with other founder-prophets. But that is no more than speculation! Every

group, to be effective, needs an identified form of leadership. This Jesus acknowledged and chose who it should be. But he was at pains to make it clear that the meaning of authority was service. He emphasised this in his own relationship with his disciplines—'I no longer call you servants but friends' (Jn. 15: 15)—and gave a dramatic example of what this is to mean in practice by washing their feet.

From these four characteristics of a religion it would be difficult to put Jesus' own movement into the category of an institutional Religion. At the end of a parable to teach his disciples 'that they should pray always and never become discouraged' he asks: 'Will the Son of Man find faith on earth when be comes?' (Lk. 18: 8): not religion, but faith.

The American theologian Thomas Sheehan is not the first to suggest that what Jesus preached was the end of religion—religion understood 'as the bond between two separate and incommensurate entities called "God" and "humanity"'—and the beginning of what religion is supposed to be about: God's presence within humanity.[9]

Are we now, in our evolution of consciousness, passing to a stage *beyond* institutionalised religion? 'Beyond', because it would serve no useful purpose as we move into the Age of the Spirit. Or are we perhaps moving towards a single multi-cultural world religion?

A global religion

Unlike the variety of Christian Churches which all sprouted from the same root—and therefore quite rightly are endeavouring to restore their unity (ecumenism)—the world's religions grew out of different cultures. Nevertheless there is also a movement abroad today for these too to draw closer together. Being a phenomenon of our times it is not unconnected with the four Key Trends we identified in Part One. There is an anxiety among religious leaders that spiritual values appear to be taking second place in our scientific times; there is a common concern that humanity is becoming increasingly out of touch and out of harmony with the spiritual forces of Mother Earth; there is a shared alarm at the lack of world peace. These common concerns are addressed by the formation of multi-religion associations—World Congress of Faith, the Temple of Understanding, etc.—by the increasing number of centres for inter-faith studies, by one-off congresses or gatherings of the world's religious leaders, as for instance the Day of Prayer for World Peace in Assisi in 1986.

9. Sheehan, T. pp. 61, 222.

In the Christian perspective, the development of inter-faith dialogue (dialogue with other world religions) is related to, and indeed demanded by the theological shift from understanding Christianity as Church-orientated to understanding our religion as Kingdom-orientated.

The Church-orientated paradigm requires that we justify the reason why we are Christians. Put crudely, it is because we consider ours to be *the* true religion, which implies a superiority over all other religions. In turn, this must include a belief that Jesus is the only Saviour and, if we are to acknowledge that God has ways of saving the majority of humankind that is not Christian, theological explanations have to be found for understanding how this can happen. And so we produce theories like 'baptism of desire' or calling members of other religions 'anonymous Christians'.

In the Kingdom-orientated paradigm the unity of humankind is uppermost, a unity derived from our having a common origin in God and a common destiny in God.

The passage of life through time is taken by different people via the different routes offered by the different religions. What is common to all religions is that they offer a meaning to life's journey and a means of reaching the ultimate destination, however that ultimate destination is understood, and in doing so, meet the deep human need for transcendence.

As the ultimate destination of all humanity is the same—expressed by the Christian in terms of the Kingdom—the Christian must accept that God acts upon human life, not despite, but through other religions. It is beyond the scope of this book to explore the tradition of uniqueness of the Christian faith and of the uniqueness of Jesus as *the* Christ. Enough to say that this is an area of exploration by contemporary theologians.[10] The reason why I am a Christian is because that particular form of religion, for which Jesus as the Christ is central, is the path that appeals to me most, being a child of Western culture. A Christian missionary today, conceiving himself or herself as a cross-cultural missionary instead of as a missionary in one direction only, going to give a superior religion to others, cannot but be in dialogue with other religious traditions. There can be no justification for intolerance since all creeds are attempts of the finite mind to grasp the infinite. Being finite, they are tentative. In the not-too-distant past religions have regarded themselves as final and absolute and have encouraged their followers to impose their creeds

---

10. See especially *No other Name?* by Paul F. Knitter. An eminently readable book on this subject. Also *The Myth of Christian Uniqueness*, Hick, J. and Knitter, P.

on the rest of the world, with disastrous results: repression, injustice and holy wars. Indeed, a great many of the 'wars' in our own time have a religious foundation: one branch of Christians against another, Christians against Moslems, one branch of Islam with another, Moslems and Christians versus Jews.

Against this backdrop is it any surprise that leaders of the world religions see that any hope of our peaceful survival as a race lies in dialogue between them?

But there is another feature of present times, again explained by the Key Trends we have identified. Until now the 'other world', and the means of reaching it, has been the dominant concern of the religions. (Little wonder Marx and others have regarded religion as escapism.) But no religion is unaffected by the story of the universe that has emerged from scientific enquiry in the last decades, nor by the realisation of the role of human consciousness in the total cosmic process. As Thomas Berry says, our discovery that the entire earth's process has been gradually altered under the influence of its most powerful single force, consciousness, is humanity's most profound revelatory experience since the great traditional religions were born. So it comes as no surprise to find the major religions represented at the United Nations as 'Non-Governmental Organisations'.

As religions become more 'earthed' in our Planet, can we then detect signs that they are drawing together and moving towards one Global Religion? All the indications would seem to point to a negative answer. Not because their members could never agree on their present disagreements but because such disagreements belong to an altogether other plane. The coming Age of the Spirit, of deeper consciousness, is calling us beyond institutionalised religion in any form. Those four characteristics of a religion that we examined—Doctrine, Moral Code, Worship and Authority Structure—all belong to the religion era of human life, not to the spiritual. They are products of and necessitated by the reasoning mind, not by the intuitive mind. Whereas any religion acceptable in the future is likely to be a 'mystical' one, giving emphasis to intuitive knowledge and for which creed and doctrine have only interpretive roles.

Frithjof Schuon sees the dividing lines between religions running not vertically between the different religions, but rather horizontally across them all. Not so much between all Christians and all Hindus but between one Christian and the next, between one Hindu and the next. The one gives priority to mystical experience over metaphysical speculation—he calls these the 'esoteric believer'—the other, whom he calls the 'exoteric believer', reverses the priority. The former have been grasped by the unity between God and creation.

The latter, which he maintains forms the bulk of the present world religious population, tend to identify the external form of their religion with the Ultimate. Incidentally, all Christian liturgy and communal prayer forms support this latter view. He believes that it is promotion of esoteric faith (or spiritual ecumenism) which will foster the unity between religions.

A Catholic theologian, Anthony Padovano, speaking at a conference on meditation in 1976 said: 'The religious response that has occurred in the Western world is a revolution that has made us more sensitive to the religions of the Orient. . . . The great turmoil in the religions is caused by the Spirit demanding interiority. Faith is not dying in the West. It is merely moving inside.'[11]

This language is strange to the ear of the Western Christian today. The Church has tended to ritualise the presence of the Spirit in the once-in-a-lifetime sacrament of Confirmation. If we can say Baptism with water is the sacrament of the Age of Pisces, perhaps we can also say Confirmation—baptism in the Spirit—is the sacrament of the Age of Aquarius. Is this why the Church has been so unsure of the place and purpose of this sacrament? The concept of the indwelling of the Holy Spirit is basic to Hindu meditation, while in Chinese religious traditions persons find their true identity in response to the Spirit active within them. The Church has a lot to learn from the religions of the East as we all enter the Age of the Spirit. But this is a matter for the Church, to which we must now apply our attention.

I should like to close this chapter on religion with a quotation from Ó Murchú which I wholeheartedly endorse:

'Formal religion in today's world has become heavily and excessively institutionalised, to such a degree that it poses a serious threat to the spiritual unfolding of humanity and the universe. The spiritual has become so fossilised in antiquated structures and liturgies that it is no longer easily identifiable for many people both inside and outside our Churches. To reawaken humanity from its spiritual torpor and indifference, to enable the species to reconnect with its spiritual roots, is one of the supreme challenges of our time.'[12]

---

11. Quoted by Ferguson. p. 405.
12. Ó Murchú, D. 1987. p. 94.

8. The Church: heading for a break-down or a break-through

With the destruction of Jerusalem and the second Temple in AD 70 by the Romans, the followers of 'The Way', as they came to be called, fled from their own country and made a cultural leap out of Judaism. The enormity of this leap taken by the small new Jewish sect, out of Palestine onto the stage of the then known world, is easily overlooked. For one thing it would seem that Jesus himself—certainly before his death and resurrection—had not foreseen that his proposed new way of living and relating should reach beyond the Jewish nation. He exhorted his contemporaries to become better Jews, to fulfil the Law of Moses. 'It is from the Jews that salvation comes', he said (Jn. 4: 22) and another time: 'Do not think that I have come to do away with the Law of Moses and the teachings of the prophets. I have not come to do away with them, but to make their teachings come true,' (Mt. 5:17).

When a pagan woman from Syro-Phoenecia begged him for a cure for her daughter he replied 'I have been sent only to those lost sheep, the people of Israel'. He did in fact grant her request because he was so amazed at her faith. (Mt. 15: 21–28) Likewise, he was astonished at the faith of the Roman Centurian who begged a cure for his servant. 'He was surprised when he heard this; he turned round and said to the crowd following him, "I tell you, I have never found faith like this, not even in Israel,"' (Lk. 7: 1–10). He was culturally conditioned to believe that God's blessings came only through the Jewish race. These incidents were a multi-racial lesson for him. He gave thanks that God was acting outside his own race.[1]

---

1. There are other verses in the Gospel (eg. Mt. 10: 18, 24: 14, 28: 19) which would seem to indicate that Jesus was expecting his disciples to preach to the Gentile world too. But we must remember that the Gospels were written years after 'The Way' had spread into Asia Minor and it is quite likely that they are not the literal words of Jesus but an interpretation of Jesus' post-resurrection understanding of his mission.

As his followers moved out of Palestine into Asia Minor they at first preached to their fellow Jews there, using the local synagogues for this purpose, then later, as the number of Gentile members grew they broke altogether with the synagogue and called themselves the *ekklesia*, the assembly, 'the Church'.

As the community grew in numbers and in geographical extent, it became institutionalised and began to show the characteristics of a religion. It began to formalise its liturgy. With the Temple destroyed there was no holy place for worship. The simple gathering of followers meeting in their homes to break bread together in the fellowship meal to celebrate the continuing presence of the Lord in their midst, became a cultic act which included the former synagogue liturgy. As the message spread it became necessary to write down different accounts of Jesus' life and teaching to assure that the true tradition was passed down. Letters were sent to different communities to explain and amplify Jesus' message—and sometimes to correct a misunderstanding. The 'Good News' announcement took on a fixed form. Eventually the Gospels and letters were collected together with two other documents to form what we call the New Testament. Organisation became necessary; overseers had to be appointed. What was 'The Way'—a new way of life—became an institution. 'Christianity' was born as a religion alongside the Jewish religion and the religion of pagan Rome. It would be influential in forming European culture for the next 1,500 years.

In the light of what we have said about the nature of religion in the last chapter we turn now to consider what is likely to be the role of the Church in the emerging New Age. This pre-supposes that there will still be need for a Church. I maintain that there will if, by 'Church', we mean an external expression of the community of Christ's followers, but, while maintaining her essential nature, she will be quite different in structure and mode of operation.

Many volumes have been written about the nature of the Church. The Second Vatican Council presented Catholics with a beautiful change in perspective from the Church as a perfect hierarchical society to the Church as the imperfect pilgrim people of God. The Council even admitted that the Church as she now exists is not the perfect Church in which we express belief in the Creed. 'This (ideal) Church', the Bishops said, 'constituted and organised in the world as a society, *subsists* in the Catholic Church' (LG. 8, DH. 1. Italics mine). But all these recent understandings of her nature are products of the old paradigm. They serve us now in our present time of transition but they are not going to be helpful for the Age of the Spirit. Already we are noticing more and more Christians—and I speak of mature

Christians, not the youth—for whom the Church in her contemporary teaching and worship is becoming irrelevant to the point at which they have arrived on their spiritual journey. Not only is the Church no longer speaking to their condition but they find that involvement in her life and liturgy is actually holding them back on the spiritual path they have set out upon. There are, for instance, increasingly more Church members who wish to deepen their contemplative prayer life but are unable to find guidance in this from their local pastors. Instead, they seek and find it outside the Christian Church in the meditation movements coming from the East.

So to answer the needs of the coming Age it is not a question of changing or building upon the model of the current paradigm but of building up an altogether new model on some very fundamental principles. We have in fact to go back again to the Gospels and start from there.

From what we saw in the last chapter we can conclude that there are very few elements which are essential to the Church by which she can still be identified as the community of followers that Jesus founded. In fact we can reduce them to four: a proclamation about a new way of living and relating (presented as the Kingdom), some specific acts by which God's spiritul gifts are bestowed (which we have come to refer to as 'sacraments'), a minimal leadership structure, and a community way of living which includes the community meal: the Eucharist or Communion. These are the non-variables. All else that we associate with Church life has evolved as needs arose in order that the essentials can be applied in practice in response to this or that culture. (It is this failure to distinguish between the essentials and their cultural expression that presents us with such vexing questions today about, for instance, the ordination of women to the priesthood and episcopate, the obligation of celibacy for priests, the use of local produce instead of 'foreign' bread and wine for the celebration of the Eucharist in Africa or in Lapland.)

We can predict that the Church of the Age of the Spirit will be recognised as a communion of the followers of Jesus the Christ. Or, as I like to describe her, as *a con-spiracy* (meaning, not a plot, but a community of those who, in its literal sense, breathe together, breathe the same Spirit) of *com-panions* (those who share the same bread—from the Latin word *panis*—those who 'break bread together').

Her emphasis will be on developing the spiritual growth of her members more through mysticism—as the experience of oneness with the ultimate reality—than through ritual. But in proportion to a greater value being attributed to personal spiritual experience, so there will be a greater need for this experience to be interpreted in the light of the revelation of Jesus. (It is our spiritual experience, after all, that makes us what we are at the moment of dying and is all we take with us into the next life.) This interpretation cannot be done by an individual but is the task of a community faithful to the Gospel.

As the Church community exercises this major role, so in turn there will continue to be the constant need for the Christian community as a whole to assess its own life against the values of the Gospel, to ensure that it continues to be the Kingdom people. The guarantee of the Risen Lord's presence with his community is given only to a faithful community, faithful to the message of Jesus. To maintain this faithfulness there will continue to be the need for 'overseers': the theologians as the 'professional thinkers' and the 'pastors' who will discern the work of the theologians and decide whether or not it is the authentic mind of the Christian community as a whole. Their authority will be that of service, a ministry to the community.

In speaking of the Kingdom in Chapter Two, I spoke of the Church as the 'focus' of the Kingdom—the Kingdom being the manifestation of God's design for the whole of humanity. This is the kernel of the Gospel message. The very fact of God's design being in the process of unfolding, of moving towards its completion, demands the presence in the world of a community that both makes that design known and also contributes towards its fulfilment by living it out in practice. This understanding of the Church's role in the New Age helps us to see how the Church will relate to other religious traditions.

The Catholic Church, in her official documents, has moved from a position of claiming that only Christianity is true and that all other religions are false, to acknowledging that truth is also found in other religions[2]. But also that the fulness of truth is not found in the Church because she is a pilgrim Church journeying towards the only absolute Truth: God[3]. The majority of Christians are no longer able to defend the thesis that the Christian tradition is superior to others, still less that it alone provides the path to salvation (although there are still some fundamentalist Christians who are vociferous in proclaiming this view and would threaten all non-Christians with eternal damnation) but they do maintain that as the Church is the sign on earth of the Kingdom, the custodian of God's revelation about his design for creation, Christians have a mission to proclaim this message to all others and to show them how much they are living

---

2. 'The Catholic Church rejects nothing which is true and holy in these religions'. Abbott, W. NA 1.
3. Abbott, W. LG 8.

the values of the Kingdom without recognising them as such. Only Christianity is able to interpret the phenomena of our times, the New Age, in the light of the Kingdom. In other words, the Church exists not to promote the Church but to promote the Kingdom of God.[4]

The Hindu philosopher, Ramanuja, uses a helpful phrase when he speaks of the world as the 'Body of God'. It reminds us of what St. Paul wrote to the Colossians, that while Christ is the head of his body, the Church, and is the source of that body's life (1: 18), God decided, through the Son, 'to bring the whole universe back to himself. God made peace through his Son's death on the cross and so brought back to himself all things, both on earth and in heaven' (1: 20). Christians, who are aware of being the Body of Christ, can regard the whole of creation potentially and in its final fulfilment, as the Body of God. The Church is the Body of Christ in order that the world may become the Body of God.

But while we can say that the Church will continue to be present in the world as the community giving a focus to the Kingdom, can we also say that she will maintain Christianity as a religion, as we have understood that word?

Let us look again at those four characteristics of formal religion to see what is happening to them as we move into the Age of the Spirit.
1. *A doctrine of beliefs, a creed.* Christian revelation is not a set of doctrines that dropped from the sky. It begins with human experience and has to be expressed and understood within the limits set by human experience. The Church's doctrine is the public statement of the Christian community's experience of the God-humanity relationship. Revelation starts from below, not from on top. That is why any form of religious education, if it is truly to convey the Gospel—which is Good News about human life— must lead people to explore their own experience.

Both interior revelation (from intuitive knowledge) and exterior revelation (from rational knowledge) are required for the growth of the full Christian life. They are mutually enriching. The former requires the exterior revelation of the Christ to interpret the inner experience. Exterior revelation without interior revelation leads to a conformist, moralist religious life, lived at surface level, without roots. Interior revelation gives it life and soul. It gives a certainty about God which requires no rational proof.

It is not our experience that is required to submit to doctrine for its validity, but the validity of our experience is given meaning

<hr>

4. For a further development of these ideas see Paul Knitter and Hick & Knitter.

by doctrine. Similarly, the purpose of Scripture is not to give us a lot of facts about God and fill our heads but to confirm the intuitive experience of God in our hearts.

The Spirit, revealing God to us through our personal experience, and the Church, are not two rivals claiming our allegiance. Jesus promised they would work in partnership: 'The Helper (the Counsellor) will come—the Spirit, who reveals the truth about God and who comes from the Father. I will send him to you from the Father, and he will speak about me. And you, too, will speak about me, because you have been with me from the beginning' (John 15: 26–27). This he said to his Apostles, the foundation members of his Church.

What is happening in our present times is that people are less prepared to accept the doctrinal authority of an outside agent— in this case the Church as she is today—without first testing it against their religious experience, to see if it rings true for them.

The wholistic paradigm that is emerging among us is seen to be nurtured more by the sciences, by secular sources, than by the official Church. The Church is finding it hard to accept this. Her response to the phenomenon is made in intellectual, theological terms instead of by giving guidance to and promoting the inner experiences that people are seeking. The growing dialogue between scientists and mystics is being initiated by the secular world and not by the Church authorities.

We have an instance of the official Church line in the field of ecumenism. Prominence is given to the intellectual discussions taking place between theologians. But that is only a fringe activity. Where real ecumenism is happening is when Christians of different Churches gather to share their deepest spiritual experiences. This is illustrated by the Catholic Church's problem over sacramental inter-communion. The official, reasoned argument is that it cannot happen until unity is achieved. In fact it is happening everywhere on the part of those who are already experiencing spiritual inter-communion and feel it is right to give this experience sacramental expression.

As Canon Peter Spink foretells: 'It is likely that as the century reaches its close, it will be the task primarily not of the theologians, but of the mystics and the new scientists to identify and articulate this change in religious consciousness, and of such, we may see Teilhard de Chardin as a great forerunner'.[5]

---

5. Spink, P. p. 16.

94

2. *A Moral code* Today we find a polarising taking place between those for whom the personal spiritual, mystical experience, is the foundation of their Christian life, their validation of the Church's truths, and, at the other end, those (often labelled 'conservatives') who are returning to the 'safety' of doctrinal pronouncements to give validation to their spiritual experience. Again, this polarising is the mark of the transition to a New Age. We notice the same thing happen at the time of transition from the Age of Aries to the Age of Pisces, 2,000 years ago. Jewish religious law had become so formalised that it had become an end in itself. Its observance was more like a tax owed to God than a means of communion with Him. Jesus set out to reverse this: to redeem us from the formalism of religion. Christians today are becoming less tolerant of rules and regulations which, being imposed from on top, appear to be originating from outside life as they experience it. The validity for moral teaching is sought today not from a hierarchical 'authority' but from its innate authenticity—because it speaks to the life situation as experienced.

In past centuries, membership of the Church and the observance of its 'rules' was understood as a necessary means to salvation. Church membership was the way to save my soul and saving my soul was conditioned by what I was allowed to do or forbidden to do. No longer. The Second Vatican Council confirmed what had already become widely accepted. Speaking of 'all men of good will in whose hearts grace works in an unseen way', the Bishops state:

> 'For, since Christ died for all men, and since the ultimate vocation of man is in fact one, and divine, we ought to believe that the Holy Spirit in a manner known only to God offers to every man the possibility of being associated with this paschal mystery'.[6]

Since, as St. Paul tells us (Rom. 5: 15,17,20) the victory of Christ was greater than the victory of Satan and since declared Christians represent only one fifth of the world's population, we have to conclude that the vast majority of human beings find their final fulfilment as a result of a life lived outside the Church, not through Church membership.

This raises the question: Why become a Church member? Merely 'to save my soul' might have been an adequate reason in the past but does not satisfy us today. One becomes a member of the Church for two reasons, one personal, the other social:

---

6. Abbott, W. GS 22.

1. to enable us to live life at a richer level;
2. to proclaim, by living life at this richer level, that it is available to all humankind.

This richer life is referred to by Jesus sometimes simply as 'life',— as when he said: 'I have come in order that you may have life— life in all its fullness' (Jn. 10: 10)—because its possession is not extra-ordinary but is meant to be the ordinary destiny of all humanity. Sometimes he refers to it as 'eternal life' by which is meant, not a life acquired and lived after death, but our participation in the God-life available already now.

Eternal life is not acquired solely by the act of our becoming members of the Church. It is potentially present in everyone (because it is the destiny of everyone) but there comes a moment when it breaks through into human life as a consciously accepted dimension. This awareness is a God-given gift, and awareness plus acceptance is referred to as the gift of Faith. We make a public affirmation of this awareness-acceptance by the act of baptism by water through which we commit ourselves to live this new-found life in the company of a faith-community and the community in turn accepts us into its membership.

The Sri Lanken theologian Tissa Balasuriya summarises what we have been saying in these words:

'The principle mission of Christians and the Churches as communities of believers is to foster the conditions for the self-realisation and fulfilment of each and every person and for the full flowering of nature'.[7]

In other words, to translate the ideal of the Kingdom into everyday terms. This forces us to ask whether the Kingdom People in the Age of the Spirit are not all those who by their life-values witness to God's Kingdom design for the whole of humanity—people who may or may not have committed themselves to be Church members—while, on the other hand, those who are not giving a Kingdom witness but would claim Church membership (on account of baptism in infancy, perhaps) are members in no more than a sociological sense?

It is not baptism that makes a person a Christian, as if it were some magical rite, but conversion to a Gospel way of living which is confirmed by Baptism as an act of entry into the Christian community, the Church. As the Jewish race was chosen to be the 'People of God' of Old Testament times to herald the coming

---

7. Balasuriya, T. p. 193

of the Christ Age, so it is the 'New People of God—the Kingdom People—who are the heralds of the Age of the Spirit. These are the people who will be baptised by the Holy Spirit, as Jesus promised (Acts 1:5; 11:16).

3. *A Way of Worship.* Worship is a characteristic of a religion because, like religion itself, it answers a human need to live in harmony with an unseen order, a Supreme Power outside and beyond our humanity. Jesus, as we have seen, while feeling that human need himself and finding it answered in the Jewish worship of Temple and Synagogue, laid down no rules for an alternative worship for his followers, but on the contrary, predicted a day when people would be offering God the worship he really wants, in spirit and in truth (Jn. 4: 19–24). Did he not say that when we pray it should be behind closed doors (Mt. 6: 5–6), in our depth?

Much of what passes for Christianity today belongs in the realm of folk religion; it simply fulfils the human desire for touching the transcendent. This is always expressed culturally. Most of our expression of Christianity in worship is cultural, not Gospel. One has only to witness an English coronation service. It is very English, very beautiful and dignified, it is uplifting. It appeals to the eye and the ear and enables our minds to transcend the work-a-day world. But what is its Gospel content?

In previous centuries 'going to church' was the only means that Christians had of receiving spiritual nourishment, apart from reading the Bible at home. Today, so many other ways are available for being spiritually instructed. While retreat houses and spiritual centres are available for the few, the masses have easy access to television and radio. Broadcasters estimate that in Britain at least 20 million adults watch or listen to a religious broadcast each week. More people listen to *The Sunday Programme* on Radio 4 than listen to *Woman's Hour*. According to audience research some of the religious radio programmes—they instance *Good Morning Sunday*—attract four times more non-church-goers than church-goers. In Gerald Priestland's phrase radio seems to have created a 'Great Church of the Unchurched'. The decline in church-going is not a measure of the spiritual life of the nation.

Faithfulness to church-going can be as destructive to spiritual growth as it can be beneficial. It can be exercised as the sum of spiritual practice so that when observed faithfully it satisfies our duty 'to take care of the soul' and deadens us to the invitation in our depths to live all aspects of life in a spiritual dimension. Church-going, as a measure of Christian life—whether as a subject for clergy statistics or as a criterion of 'practising'—is a false factor. If it is expected as a minimum requirement of Christian practice, it is also regarded by many as the maximum.

Church-going, however, in the sense of large numbers of people assembling anonymously in their local church on Sundays, will continue to be a declining practice in proportion to the growth in popularity of the smaller, more personal unit, the house-church or Basic Christian community. The *ecclesia*—meaning 'people called together'—of the New Age will be this eucharistic neighbourhood community, while the 'parish'—made up of two Greek words meaning 'beside' and 'house'—will be the multi-faith neighbourhood in which the Kingdom life will be lived and shared and woven.

But let me return to the evolution of worship in the context of the New Age of consciousness. While the need for placating and honouring a God as a distant, all-powerful Being is found in many world religions, it is precisely in this that Christianity ought to be different, since through Jesus Christians are raised to a new filial relationship with God, as adopted sons and daughters whose prayer is 'Abba'. In point of fact, the form Christian worship takes today, drawing from Old Testment scriptures and in particular the psalms, reinforces a pre-Christian relationship with God. It is curious to note today the divide among Christians caused by their different understanding of the Eucharist: between those who regard the Eucharist principally as a sacrifice and those who regard it as a meal in the fellowship of the risen Lord. The fundamental question we find ourselves faced with, and upon the answer to which we build our understanding of and attitude towards worship, is whether worship is something we do for God or for our own benefit.

St. Paul, in the first days of the Church already, begs his Roman community to interiorise their worship:

'Because of God's great mercy to us I appeal to you: Offer yourselves as a living sacrifice to God, dedicated to his service and pleasing to him. This is the true worship that you should offer. Do not conform yourselves to the standards of this world, but let God transform you inwardly by a complete change of your mind. *Then* you will be able to know the will of God— what is good and is pleasing to him and is perfect' (Rom. 12: 1–2).

That word *then* is crucial. Teachers of asceticism in the past have taught that it is by works of penance, self-sacrifice, self-control

that we draw nearer to God. Paul is saying that our unity with
God will come about because we have let God transform us
inwardly.

The Age of the Spirit will see 'worship' in the life of the
Christian taking two complementary forms. On the one hand,
there will be an increase of mystical prayer, principally through
the practice of deep meditation, which liberates the inbuilt drive
or impulse towards transcendence and unity which is in every
human being. On the other hand, because we also have an inbuilt
drive towards relationships, there will be the regular gathering
of Christians around the Eucharistic table to celebrate as a
community their union with God in daily life, through Jesus, and
the promise of the fullness of life to which they, along with the
whole of humanity, are journeying.

4. *An authority structure.* It is not our purpose here to draw up a
blueprint for the shape of the Church of the New Age. We are
concerned with *what* the Church will be, not *how* she will operate.
As with any human group there will be those who are called upon
to exercise a leadership role and to provide different ministries
to and on behalf of the community. But they will be drawn from
the community as the need arises and the shape of the structure
and the form of leadership will differ from culture to culture
instead of having one universal administrative model as at present.

The Church, as she is structured today, will neither disappear
suddenly nor change radically on account of any re-formation
originating from within. It is the way of institutions that as they
cease to be relevant they do not immediately close up shop but
they continue to exist along an increasingly sterile track,
maintained by those for whom they are an anchor-point and safe
mooring against the violence of change in other aspects of life.
Arnold Toynbee remarks that during the disintegration of a
civilization, two separate plays with different plots are being
performed simultaneously side by side. In the case of the Church,
there are several reasons why this should be so. First, because
her spiritual nature gives her a transcendent value on account of
which many members will maintain her as a defence against the
increasing secularisation of our age. Secondly, because Jesus'
promise that he would be with his followers till the end of time
(Mt. 28: 20) is interpreted by most members—and especially by
the leadership—as applying to the institution of Church as they
know it.

Thirdly, because it is not widely appreciated, either by the

Church hierarchy or by the majority of her members, that it is not the task of hierarchical authority to initiate change but to maintain the Christian community in orthodoxy and unity. Communities are not being open to the Spirit if they sit back and wait for change to be commanded from above. In the whole of Church history major change has never been initiated from the top but has always sprung from movements at the grass-roots, which have later been either condemned or approved by the hierarchy.

In the last chapter we showed what a high percentage of people, irrespective of their religious affiliation, have had some sort of spiritual, mystical experience. David Hay reveals an intriguing fact in his analysis of one of the opinion polls made in Britain.[8] He gives a breakdown of those who have had such an experience according to their denominations:

Anglicans	33%
Jews	39%
Roman Catholics	41%
Other non-Christians	60%
Other Christians	68%

It would appear that the less people are bound to a hierarchical Church, the more open they seem to be to mystical experience! But perhaps it is not so surprising. Ever since the 2nd Century the hierarchical leadership of the Church has had difficulties in handling its faithful—in those early days, the Gnostics—who claimed to possess an 'inside', mystical knowledge. Geddes MacGregor, writing of the Gnostics, says: 'Their teaching was probably the major cause of the Church's hardening itself into an institute with a more rigid doctrinal system and a more orderly ecclesiastical structure than Christians had generally found necessary in the first century'. 'The history of Christian thought is peppered with warnings and protests against the dangers of the mystical tradition that has developed within the Church'.[9] Is the fact of the growing religious experience in our own day related to the diminution of the influence of hierarchical authority? The leadership of the Church of the future will be modelled less on the shepherd who is intent upon keeping his flock following along closely together, than on the fisherman encouraging his crew to launch into the deep.

---

8. Hay, D. p. 125.
9. pp. 1, 5.

With the evermore rapid transition into the Age of the Spirit—the transcendental age—the present structured organisation of the Church will become increasingly obsolete. It will not disappear by intent but simply fade into irrelevance. The essence of Church, however, as being the communion of the followers of Jesus the Christ, will continue his mission to the world. Karol Wojtyla, before his election as the present Pope John Paul II, wrote while he was still a bishop in Poland: 'The Church can share in the evolution of the world only on this essential condition: that is to say through its own evolution'[10].

---

10. Wojtyla, K. p. 174.

9. 'Deliver us from all that is evil'

Perhaps one of the mental shifts consequent upon the emergence of the New Age of the Spirit which is causing people most difficulty—in particular to the traditional Christian—is that regarding the experience of evil in our world and in our personal lives and how we are to understand our dependence on God's power to be delivered from it. Here we will deal with four aspects of evil—evil experienced as suffering, evil as negativity, evil expressed as sin, and evil expressed as a blockage to growth. In the following chapter we will look at the different ways of understanding what we call 'Redemption' from evil.

Evil experienced as suffering

We never experience evil as evil in our lives but experience its effect which is suffering. Suffering is alien to human life and therefore since human life first appeared—since humanity with the ability to reflect upon its experience first appeared—a fundamental human question has been: why are we caused to suffer? What is the source of the evil that causes our suffering? All cultures have invented their own myth to answer this question, some believing that it orginates, prior to human creation, in a battle between rival gods. Siva, one of the three great gods of Hinduism is the god of destruction as well as of creation. These myths are a way of coping with something which humanity unaided feels unable to overcome.

Since evil is experienced by us as suffering, it is helpful to consider that the causes of suffering are two-fold. There are those sufferings that enter our lives from sources extraneous to ourselves and others which originate from within our own depth.

Among the first category we can list the following:

— Disease: although great strides are being made to eradicate their causes, eg. TB., Malaria, but new ones appear: AIDS.
— Accidents, and accidental death: we have not sufficiently mastered the machines we have invented.
— 'Nature': earthquakes, floods, droughts, wild animals.

- Hurt inflicted by other human beings: physical (wounding, war, violence, torture, imprisonment, etc.) or mental (their hatred, envy, revenge, greed, etc.) or hereditary (children of alcoholics inheriting the disease).
- Bodily weakness: hunger, fatigue, excesses of heat or cold and ultimately the suffering of debility in old age.

These sufferings are experienced by all of us on account of our human condition. By taking on our human condition Jesus too was open to experiencing these forms of suffering. They are not in themselves moral evils but may be the consequence of other people's moral evils.

The other cause of suffering finds its roots within each one of us because of our own slaveries from which we are unable to break entirely free. St. Paul spoke of it this way: 'I do not understand what I do; for I don't do what I would like to do, but instead I do what I hate' (Rom. 7: 15). Among these slaveries would be:

- my pride: having to defend a false self, pretending to be who I am not. Not accepting my own limitations.
- my possessiveness: defending what I *have* or battling to obtain what I desire to have draws off energy that should be spent on my *being* more.
- my insecurity: the fear of letting go. Ultimately of the final let-go, the fear of dying. The most crippling of fears, however, is not of death but that there is no meaning to life.

Our concern here is with this second category, what we call moral evil, because it arises from a human choice. It is not a form of suffering found in the animal kingdom. All the great religions offer ways of breaking down the barrier within us which keeps us enchained in these slaveries: the barrier between our inside selves and our outside selves, between what we wish we were and what we actually are: between what we actually are and what God created us to become. We will be seeing in the following chapter how Jesus, who was completely true to his real self, having no contradiction between his outer and his inner person, but being completely whole (holy), empowers us to break through our personal barriers.

Evil as negativity

The contradictory thing about evil is that it is. . . . and it is not. In the Bible and in literature generally evil has been associated with darkness. Darkness makes a good comparison because it is something we are acutely aware of by the way it affects, indeed limits, our ability.

Yet asked what darkness is we can do no more than describe it negatively, as an absence of light, because we never actually encounter darkness as something having its own existence. Similarly, evil has no existence as an entity in itself. It is the shadow side of what is created. All that is created is positive because it issues from God, is a reflection of God. Not so evil. It occurs when energies are expended negatively, as when the energies that are for the building up of the human family are diverted into oppression, injustice, and selfishness. It is an energy turned inside out. Yet there are times when its influence is felt so strongly that we can be excused for giving it substance, even for personalising it. As when Jesus came to the point in his life when he had to turn his face to Jerusalem and encounter the Jewish authorities and Peter tried to dissuade him:

'From that time on Jesus began to say plainly to his disciples, "I must go to Jerusalem and suffer much from the elders, the chief priests, and the teachers of the Law. I will be put to death, but three days later I will be raised to life". Peter took him aside and began to rebuke him. "God forbid it, Lord!" he said. "That must never happen to you!" Jesus turned around and said to Peter, "Get away from me, Satan! You are an obstacle in my way, because these thoughts of yours don't come from God but from man".' (Mt. 16: 21–23)

The effects of evil can be so overwhelming that we seek to escape from our personal moral responsibility by putting blame on to some force outside ourselves. Early cultures developed a whole system of devils or evil spirits as an explanation for the destructive powers within them with which they felt unable to cope. When I was living in Zambia I remember reading of a court case in which a teacher was being accused of stealing hens. His plea was: 'I didn't do it. It was an eivl spirit within me that did it'.

Evil is not of God's creation, it is of our own creation. We give it substance, being, by believing in it as having an existence of its own. When we express belief in something—make an act of faith in something—we not only concede reality to it but we surrender a part of ourselves to it, we give it part of our own being. To confess a belief in God is to put myself under the power of God. To give credence to evil is to allow its influence and control.

Much is written of evil, and of the personification of evil, in both Old and New Testaments, showing us how evil was explained in that culture at that time. Although no Christian Creed has ever required us to believe *in* evil, the Church is constantly bringing it to our minds. The present Fall-Redemption theological paradigm causes us to stress more the negativity within us than all that is positive and good and up-building. It is no surprise that some theologians today are questioning the meaning of the doctrine of Original Sin. The concept is not a Jewish one. Herbert Haag, former president of the Catholic Bible Association of Germany and author of *Is Original Sin in the Scripture?* writes:

'The doctrine of original sin is not found in any of the writings of the Old Testament. It is certainly not in Chapters one to three of Genesis. This ought to be recognised today, not only by Old Testament scholars, but also by dogmatic theologians.'
'The idea that Adam's descendents are automatically sinners because of the sin of their ancestor, and that they are already sinners when they enter the world, is foreign to Holy Scripture.'[1]

and we might add, foreign to human instinct, to mothers of newly born babies especially. Christian liturgy and hymns are constantly reminding us of our misery, our worthlessness 'as banished children of Eve, mourning and weeping in this veil of tears' and undermining any self confidence we try to build upon as accepted sons and daughters of God loved infinitely by him. No wonder people accuse Christians of being pre-occupied with sin!

Evil is a negation. The most powerful of all weapons against evil is to refuse to give it a place in our consciousness. This is not the same as saying we cannot have opinions *about* evil: that is an intellectual exercise, such as we are engaged upon in our present considerations. It is like the difference between having opinions *about* God, as an atheist has, and believing *in* God which implies a faith commitment *to* God. The latter operates at a different level of consciousness.

I must confess to a feeling of unease at healing sessions conducted by some groups of Charismatic Christians. They so concentrate in searching out evil, whether in places or persons, that they seem to attract to themselves the very forces they seek to combat. They give substance to evil. The most effective weapon against evil is to give evil no credence, no substance but instead to give substance to what is positive as St. Paul urges the Christians in Philippi: 'Fill your minds with those things that are good and that deserve praise: things that are true, noble, right, pure, lovely, and honourable' (4: 8). We act from the level of our consciousness and the level at which Jesus acted was to deny that evil had any place in God's Kingdom. 'Jesus appears to have proclaimed a world in which we will be delivered from the

---

1. p. 19 and p. 106.

consciousness and even the very concept of sin'.[2] For a long time I have felt that the phrase in the Lord's Prayer—'deliver us from evil'—is a shorthand rendering of 'deliver us from all that is evil', where 'evil' is used as an adjective, not as a noun.

Evil expressed as sin

The reader will have noticed that our point of departure in this chapter is evil, not sin; evil as negativity, the denial of what is good, wholesome, harmonic. In our Christian tradition we are accustomed to the word 'sin' as a way to understand evil within a framework in which unity is expressed in terms of relationships held together by love. To sin is explained as to sever or damage our relationship with God which usually occurs through damaging our relationship with other people.

Humanity's understanding of sin has evolved in stages. In the Old Testament it is understood against a background in which it was believed that God had commanded a certain pattern within the framework of which life was to be lived. To step outside was to become ritually impure, to stay within the limits one was ritually clean and would consequently be the recipient of God's blessings. This applied to the tribe as a whole and to the individual only as a member of the tribe. A Covenant was made with the tribe, not with individuals. One individual harming another did not bring down the wrath of God unless the boundaries laid down were over-stepped. Evil was sin when it offended God, not because it harmed a neighbour. Furthermore, God was offended, sin was committed, even when the boundaries were over-stepped unwittingly without any personal moral guilt as we understand it now. Justification was achieved by a strict observance of the exterior law with little regard for the internal dispositions.

Jesus had a hard time to convince his fellow Jews that 'it is not what goes into a person's mouth that makes him ritually unclean; rather, what comes out of it makes him unclean' (Mt. 15: 10) and he had harsh words for 'the teachers of the law and the Pharisees' who maintained the people in this understanding (Mt. 23). Paul continued this battle—chiefly in his letter to the Church in Rome—trying to deliver the early Christians from believing that it was the external observance of the law which gained them justification.

Even today, the word 'sin' for most Christians is associated with

2. Cupitt, D. 1982. p. 98.

having done something wrong, with having broken a commandment or law. We think of 'sin' rather than 'sinfulness', of things we
are forbidden to do rather than as a state of being. The expression
'living in sin' has come to have an exclusively sexual connotation.
And yet if we go back to its etymology it really describes a state.
The New Testament Greek word for sin is *hamartia* which is an
archery term meaning to miss the target: to live off-target. This more
nearly describes what Jesus meant by the word. His final words to
the woman caught in adultery: 'Go, but do not sin again' (Jn. 8: 11)
are surely not an expectation that she will never do wrong again,
but an admonition to a conversion, to a change of direction in her
life, 'do not be off target anymore'. It is the state of sinfulness which
is the cause of acts of sin. It is a state of sickness of mind, of a
disharmony in a person, which is in need of healing, of making whole
again.

When a tree is diseased it is revealed in the withering of its leaves.
The cure does not lie in washing the leaves but in giving the right
nourishment to the root. A person is cured of a state of sin, not by
attacking the deeds by which it is manifested, but by attending to
their blockages or weakness so as to establish him or her in wholeness.
This has an important lesson for us. For many centuries, until
recently, writers on asceticism have proposed exercises in
mortification, abnegation and self-control as a means of acquiring
holiness or wholeness. This has directed the energies to curing the
leaves, as it were. Today, with a regained understanding of our human
make-up and the return to a wholistic approach to life, we are
appreciating that it is in the bringing to maturity of the whole person
by the cultivation of their deeper consciousness that the manifestations
will be healed. I have already pointed out the importance of the little
word *then* in Rom. 12: 2. Paul makes the same point to the Colossians:
'We ask God to fill you with the knowledge of his will, with all the
wisdom and understanding that his spirit gives. *Then* you will be
able to live as the Lord wants and will always do what pleases him'
(1: 9–10). Only by living in closer unity with the divine, creative
mind, can we integrate our divided selves and become whole. To
the Christians in Ephesus St. Paul says: 'Your hearts and minds must
be made completely new, and you must put on the new self which
is created in God's likeness and reveals itself in the true life that is
upright and holy' (4: 23–24). The 'new self' is the real Self that
God created each of us to be and our task in this life is to discover
that real Self, our true identity.

This understanding provides an interesting meeting point between
two great religious philosophies. In the Judeo-Christian tradition of
the Western world sin is understood as a damaging of relationships

(with God, with fellow human beings) and is healed by a growth in love, the cement of relationships. In the oriental religions what we call sin is caused by ignorance. 'Ignorance' is understood not as a lack of knowledge of facts but as a lack of integrity due to a deficient consciousness. The bridge between the two philosophies lies in the word 'harmony'. The path to pure consciousness is one of increasing harmony both of all the faculties that go to make up the Self and of the Self with the environment, with the forces of evolving creation. Harmony is the experience of right relationships.

Evil expressed as a blockage to growth

The New Age of consciousness is giving birth to a further development of our understanding of evil. As it is becoming harder to think of God as a person 'out there' who has imposed a set of rules upon humanity, so it is more difficult to think of evil as a breaking of these rules. If we are now relating to God at the centre of our being—of all being—as the creative, life-giving force, then evil will be conceived of as anything which becomes an obstacle or barrier to the free flow of this force. In other words, evil is that which is destructive or preventive of growth, whether one's own or other people's.[3] And in our wholistic perspective we can add, that which prevents the well-being, the growth and the full flowering of our universe: that which prevents the free flow of creative, evolutionary energy throughout the world.

Even if we cannot accept the imposition of arbitrary rules we must nevertheless accept that creation is governed by a law, it is the Law of Nature: the framework which brings about the harmony of all creation. The Law of Nature is the law of growth, providing the conditions for all beings to develop their full potential. For us human beings this potential is, as St. Paul tells us, to grow to the full stature of the Christ (Eph. 4:13) as Jesus did. Everything that prevents that is contrary to the divine Will, is a negativity. If evil is a denial of growth, a negativity, a non-creation, how did it originate?

Evil, as distinct from disaster, has its origins in humanity. I would suggest that it has its origins in the human person's search for identity. This search is a peculiarity of the human species because only the human person, being self-reflective, has need of an identity. We are born without a self-identity. We acquire awareness of our identity through the way we are treated by others. We blossom, we grow, to the extent that we are loved and so can recognise ourselves as the

---

3. Since writing this chapter I have encountered Scott Peck's *People of the Lie* in which many similar ideas are developed.

object of love. We appreciate ourselves to the degree that we experience our worth, as somebody worth loving. Love is the seed bed of growth. In the measure that we are deprived of love we are hampered in our growth. Since the love we receive from others is imperfect, lacking complete altruism, we make up for its deficiency by our own struggle for identity. Such a struggle, born of an imperfection, leads us along false paths to growth, along paths to self-centredness.

A few examples of these false paths will illustrate how they become destructive of growth. Persons whose self-appreciation is deficient may become dependent for their identity on their roles—as parent, as manager, as husband or wife, as shop steward, as bar attendant, as civil servant, as vicar—seeking to be recognised through the exercise of the authority or responsibility that such roles give. The greatest personal damage caused by unemployment is that with their loss of roles people lose the identity they mistakenly placed in those roles. They felt they were valued for what they did or what they produced rather than for what they are as persons. Sadly, the structure of Western society encourages this misplaced value. Another false path is in believing that recognition comes through acquiring possessions, be they material goods, titles or by being possessive of other human beings. Or again, in thinking that one can only be "someone" by being contrasted with other people: that one can only grow in proportion to one's ability to belittle others. Such a person tries to acquire notice by pulling others down, as the only way to reach the top of the human pyramid. Power-seeking, whether as individuals, families, clans, industries or nations is the most common false means of establishing a personal, or group identity. War is the evil outcome.

Each of these paths leads to evil when there is a struggle for personal growth by means of diminishing or preventing the growth of others. Preventing growth is the essence of evil. The initial struggle for identity of our first ancestors began to produce a collective evil and each human being is born into this collective evil which is why the love we receive is never perfect enough to obviate the need for each of us in turn to choose a false path. To follow a false path is to go against the current, the natural flow of creative energy, and that creates stress.

Stress: an impediment to growth

We must distinguish between stress and tension. We need to live in a state of tension. Tension produces human energy, otherwise we become zombies, we become listless. Tension is like a wound spring within us which exerts energy. In Yoga our energy drive is symbolised by *Kundalini*, a coil with three and a half turns. In Hindu symbolism it is sometimes represented as a serpent coiled at the base of the spine. But stress is the over-loading of the nervous system to the point of disintegration.

Today we are realising more and more the destructive effect of stress in our lives. Medical people are acknowledging that stress is the fundamental cause of a great many illnesses. Priests and ministers are perceiving that it is at the root of a great deal of the evil that religious people confess as sin.

While many doctors are feeling the inappropriateness of simply prescribing medicine for a physical ailment but are turning to the healing of the whole person, the spiritual as well as the mental and physical, and prescribing alternative forms of healing which often include deep meditation, priests are arriving at the same conclusion from the other direction, realising the inadequacy of a two-minute ritual absolution in the confessional for spiritual dis-ease without taking into account and helping people to be released from personal and social stresses that are enchaining them in their situation of sinfulness.

Virus-caused disease	The grey area of multiple cause	Devil-caused dis-ease
———————————————→	←———————————————	
Purely physical 'cure' for the present	Wholistic 'treatment'. Release of inner healing power	Exorcism or sacramental forgiveness for the past

Convergence in healing

Neither the doctor nor the priest actually heals. The healing originates in the creative power, the source of life, in the depth of each person. What the 'healer' does—whether by medicine or prayer or sacrament—is to enable that healing power to be released. Healing is not essentially release from suffering but rather an aid to growth. (No one can be healed of old age because at that stage of life the inner creative power is diminishing.)

There is a shift today from 'curing sickness in order to get well again' to 'healing as a means to becoming whole' and one of the principle means of this latter is to deal with stress. The pace and pressures of our Western way of life impose unmanageable levels of stress on the human person.

'Neurotic, off-centred parents in an alienated, off-centred society must almost by definition produce neurotic, alienated, off-centred children. Not only will they be sinners in the general sense of living in a state of disconnectedness from God, but the very nature of a highly stressed society is an inducement to false goals, meaningless ambitions, wrong desires and therefore sin in the sense of moral weakness, the inability to choose right, the inability to let go of obsessive self-concern. And yet we all know of people who live in radiant serenity in the midst of the urban darkness. They may not even profess any formal faith, but they invariably are people who radiate a wholeness, a holiness which proclaims louder than any overtly pious behaviour their connectedness with the Spirit'.[4]

Today a growing number of people are finding that the twice-daily practice of deep meditation is the new salvific, healing grace in their lives. It has an integrating, harmonising effect on the whole human system reducing the level of stress and making the person more able to contain and absorb the impact of stress from outside. It puts a person in touch with the creative, healing, 'redeeming' forces of life, with the power at the inner-centre of their being where the Spirit touches them, which no number of virtuous actions will ever do. New life begins to flow, not by adding a new ingredient, but by the removal of a barrier to awareness of our true worth in God's eyes.[5]

It would be a mistake to suppose that this new understanding of evil, because it departs from traditional Christian language, calls into question our dependence on God, the source of creative power, to rise above our present state. Alone we are powerless. We have to be attracted to and empowered to grow in the life of the Spirit by the Spirit of the Christ himself. Still in the Christian perspective, we have to ask ourselves if it is possible to offer an explanation, in the context of this new understanding, of how the historical event of the life, death and resurrection of Jesus the Christ, two thousand years ago, relates to the personal struggle of each of us to grow to our full potential. This I will now attempt.

4. O'Brien, A. p. 66.
5. Watson, L. 1987. p. 131.

10. 'Redemption': looking backward or looking forward

When drafting this chapter I thought of entitling it 'I don't want to be saved: I want to grow' because to me that sums up the difference in our religious attitude between the paradigm of the Age of Jesus the Christ and that of the Age of his Spirit. Salvation looks backwards, while growth looks forward, at the continually creating Spirit of Jesus, as the following diagram shows.

1. Redemption as backward-looking:

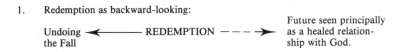

Undoing ◄────── REDEMPTION ── ── ► Future seen principally
the Fall   as a healed relation-
                                                   ship with God.

2. 'Redemption' as forward-looking:

Gradual rise in
awareness
of human   "REDEMPTION"   An elevation to the
potential   potentials of the
                                        Kingdom: empowered to
                                        reach our total fulfil-
                                        ment

Before we can develop these ideas we need to clarify our terminology. This in turn causes us to face the question I posed at the end of the previous chapter. *How* do we explain in a way that is meaningful today *what* it was that the Christ effected for human nature that empowers humanity to reach its full potential? How stuck are we with the Church's traditional explanation and terminology, considering that this doctrine is at the very heart of Christian belief?

Strangely enough it is precisely because belief in the Christ's 'saving' act is at the centre of Christian teaching that it has never been challenged. It has never been found necessary to define what is meant by the Redemption with any degree of precision.

112

The occasions for dogmatic definitions by the Church have been the appearance of ideas that have been considered to be heretical. This is why so many Church dogmas appear to put a disproportionate weight on one aspect. They were historically conditioned and framed to explain a particular point of a doctrine that was being attacked. But this has not occurred in the case of the doctrine of Redemption or Atonement as the eminent theologian John Macquarrie reminds us:

> 'The Church has never formulated a doctrine of atonement with the same precision with which it has tried to define the person of Christ. Instead, we find several explanatory models that have developed side by side. Even in the New Testament a considerable variety of ways of understanding the atoning work of Christ is to be found'.[1]

Dietrich Weiderkehr, in his book *Belief in Redemption* laments the irrelevancy of historical concepts about the Christ's redeeming act and the terminology which is still used and proposes that the Church should undertake 'a radical revision of belief in redemption'. He speaks of 'the epochal gap or divide between traditional belief in redemption and man's quest (both explicit and implicit) for salvation today'.[2] This is not the place to make an historical survey of the way in which the belief has developed, but it is useful to mention a few key ideas. To the young Christians of New Testament times brought up in the Jewish tradition it made sense to give an explanation in terms of the Fall and Salvation. This language was unhelpful in another cultural and religious environment that was unfamiliar with Jewish mythology. But God has done something through Jesus for the benefit of the whole human race. So another explanation had to be found that spoke to the Gentiles as well. Among a people to whom religious sacrifice was commonplace the sacrifical nature of the Christ-event was a perfectly satisfactory explanation.

'Sacrifice' is not a word used much today in Western society and yet it is one of the chief features of any ancient religion.

As people of former societies offered gifts to chiefs and kings to obtain their help or plead for their mercy—or simply to pay homage— it was thought fitting to offer gifts for the same purpose to the unseen rulers of the universe. And since these latter were the source of life, what better gift than a life—preferably a human life or, as a substitute, the life of a bull or a goat or a valued animal? What could be a more

---

1. Macquarrie, J. pp. 314–315.
2. p.x.

fitting sacrifice to make reparation to the supreme God, giver of all life, than the sacrifice of the most highly valued life in creation: the human life of his son? St. Peter uses this argument: 'You know what was paid to set you free from the worthless manner of life handed down by your ancestors. It was not something that can be destroyed, such as silver or gold; it was the costly sacrifice of Christ, who was like a lamb without defect or flaw' (I Peter 1: 18–19). This *explanation* carries little persuasion for us today, in a culture which no longer worships—nor even honours its temporal rulers—with sacrifices. Indeed such would be referred to as a bribe! Hence, incidentally, the anachronism today of perpetuating the explanation of the Eucharist as a sacrifice. But back to the first days of the Church.

She was smarting from the blow caused by the seemingly meaningless manner and fact of the untimely death of Jesus. Meaning must be found for it. So a cultic, priestly theory of atonement was soon developed.[3] His 'sacrifice on Calvary' became the central, and in some cases, unique location of Jesus' saving action. We notice the train of thought develop from 'was it not necessary?' (Lk. 24: 26) through 'the Scriptures must be fulfilled' (Mk. 14:49) to the significance of Jesus' death as a redeeming act (Mk. 10:45). '*Bestowing* meaning *on* the cross by appealing to God's salvific activity, Jesus' own intentions and the salvific efficacy of Calvary came unconsciously to be mistaken for an inner *possession* of meaning *by* the passion and cross, even by the death itself'[4]. Jesus never gave a value to suffering as such, he never condoned it. He recognised its purifying effect but he would not accept it as part of God's plan. It was a negation of God's desire for our happiness—even on this earth. The majority of his miracles were done to relieve people from it. He was even impatient with it, healing on the sabbath without waiting till the next day.

While the Eastern Churches regarded the incarnation as the decisive saving action, the Western Church continued to regard the death of Jesus as the pivot of salvation, interpreting it almost exclusively as sacrifice and atonement. The theory of Jesus making 'satisfaction' for sin, proposed by St. Anselm of Canterbury, dominated the Middle Ages and greatly influenced such great theologians as St. Thomas Aquinas. If humanity's infinite guilt, the latter argued, was not to be merely overlooked in God's mercy but actually removed, there had to be satisfaction which could only be made by a human being

---

3. Brueggemann, W. p. 91.
4. Weiderkehr, D. p. 31.

of divine, infinite worth. In terms almost of a commercial deal, this saving act was concentrated on the death of Jesus. One might be forgiven for thinking that God demanded his son's death.

That St. Paul had linked death with resurrection as the saving event seems to have been lost sight of for a great part of the Church's history in the West. Until a revival of resurrection theology in the 1960's the resurrection was valued as no more than the ultimate proof of Jesus' divinity. But only more recently still has the totality of Jesus' life, his preaching and healing, been given salvific value. Previously the rest of his life was valued only as providing a model for Christian living. 'The life of Jesus either unfolded the redemption that had already been brought by the incarnation (for Eastern Christians) or merely led up to the all-sufficient sacrifice of his cross' (for Western Christians).[5]

These various expressions of a price requiring to be paid seem to be quite a departure from Jesus' own understanding of God's way of forgiving. In the parable of the prodigal son the father did not demand a blood sacrifice to appease his sense of justice before welcoming his son back as one of the family. The father took the initiative and expressed forgiveness just as soon as the son was seen to be returning. Again, in the Lord's Prayer the only condition required for receiving God's forgiveness is that we be prepared to forgive others equally gratuitously. The redeeming act in both cases is the healing of a severed relationship.

Today, with our social conscience awakened, we notice how very individualistic was the Church's traditional teaching on salvation. The emphasis was on its spiritual value for the individual and the person's concern with the after-life. It was about the way our 'soul' was saved and how that salvation would be experienced in heaven. It had little to say about the 'salvation' or uplifting of the totality of human life nor about the cosmic or even social effect of 'redemption'.

This traditional teaching does not address today's concerns where people have a greater sense of offending their fellow human beings than of offending God, where we define ourselves in relation to other people rather than in direct relation to God.

Nor do we find another traditional explanation helpful: that Jesus 'took our place', suffered punishment 'on our behalf'. This concept of representation or substitution—what is called in theology 'vicarious atonement'—where one person can take on the actions of another, or the guilt of another, is less comprehensible for us today in a world

---

5. Weiderkehr, D. p. 15.

where people want to be more participative themselves. Today we are inclined to give less value to a static concept of 'salvation', as an historical event, but appreciate more the dynamic role of the Spirit in making the liberating Christ perpetually present to us and active within us.

So long as the Church continues to use the terminology of early Christianity and of the Middle Ages—using expressions like 'salvation', 'redemption', taken from the era of slavery: 'Now you have been set free from sin and are the slaves of God' (Rom. 6:22), 'atonement', 'satisfaction', 'being saved by the Blood of the Lamb'—it will be hard for people not of this tradition to appreciate the value of the Christ-event for their everyday lives. Weiderkehr concludes his book by saying: 'The Church's theology and praxis must alter their stance and approach the ever-changing human reality because of new experiences, in particular new experiences of sin and expectations of salvation. Man's search for salvation and the Church's testimony to salvation no longer, alas, coincide'.[6]

And so we find our contemporaries asking how the act of a person (in this case the life, death and resurrection of Jesus) two thousand years ago can affect their lives today.

Let us attempt an understanding of the Christ-event which is not looking backwards but looking forwards; which is not in terms of paying debts, redeeming or saving but of offering the potential for growth.

Until this century Christian doctrine has explained the Redemption as the redeeming from a fallen state. But another way of understanding the early days of humanity is gaining ground as an explanation which is more in keeping with what we are discovering about the human evolution. Instead of looking back to restoring a glorious past it understands the human journey as one which is ever moving forwards. In brief, the thinking follows these lines.

The evolution of consciousness of humanity as a whole is epitomised in the gradual development of consciousness within each human person's life.

Some psychologists[7] divide the mental growth process of humanity into three stages: the sub-conscious, the self-conscious and the super-conscious. The first is the pre-personal, sub-conscious stage in which the emerging human was one with the animal kingdom: the hunting, gathering era before there was any verbal communication

---

6. p. 90.
7. This notion is expounded at length by Ken Wilber in his book *Up from Eden*.

among the species, before the human being had the ability to think and so to differentiate itself from its natural surroundings. There was no consciousness of self present which would have given the human being an identity. It was a state of oneness with nature, with no differentiation: a 'Paradise' of harmony. This is the state of the baby in the womb, where ignorance is bliss. To grow, to attain a consciousness and an identity the baby has to go through the experience of being expelled from that Paradise and in passing into the world of consciousness, experiences the pain of separateness and individuation. The biblical description of Eden is a description of this primeval oneness with all nature. The biblical Fall is the painful step into a state of self-consciousness. Self-consciousness allows for self-determination, for choice, which opens the way to the experience of good and evil: tasting the fruit of 'the tree of knowledge of good and evil'.

As in our birth, the pain of loss of the security of the womb (Eden) was the price to be paid for moving into a higher state of humanisation. This breakthrough into the state of the 'early mind' allowed the development of thought, of verbal communication, of conscious relating to the earth and to other human beings, of the ability to think in terms of a past and a future (and consequently of planning for that future and therefore the move from being a hunter, gatherer to being a farmer).

Humanity is still in this second evolutionary stage of self-consciousness but to a more developed degree. As we have said in a previous chapter, there are signs today that humanity is passing into the third great era, that of super-consciousness, which is the destiny of each of us as individuals—in the 'next life' if not already in this—as it is for the whole of humanity.

Parallel with this scientific theory increasingly more biblical scholars today are in agreement that the Genesis account of the Garden of Eden is not describing a perfect state that has been lost to humanity but a primitive state of innocence because of ignorance. When Adam and Eve ate of the tree of knowledge of good and evil they lost their 'innocence' by acquiring knowledge—of space, time and personality. The Fall was not a falling *from* a perfect state to a damaged state but the first glimmer of an understanding of their falling *short* of the tremendous possibilities that were offered to them. The point St. Paul is making in his letter to the Romans is not that it is Adam who is held up as the model or perfection of humanity but Jesus the Christ, the person who lived in super-consciousness in unity with God[8].

---

8. Murphy-O'Connor, J. p. 44.

One hears it said that 'the modern cult of self-realisation' and the quest to fulfil one's human possibilities goes counter to the spirit of the Gospels which invite us to go the way of the Cross. Yet the Catholic Bishops of England and Wales, in their document *The Easter People* remind us 'that redemption necessarily involves the struggle to achieve full human development' (167). A great many Christians are unable to accept that God wants nothing else but our happiness *even in this present life*. So many have deep within them a sneaking feeling that if life feels good it cannot be quite right because it is our lot to suffer. It is in fact our lot to suffer but not because it is God's will for us. I have already mentioned how Jesus compaigned to relieve people of suffering. That we do suffer in the ways we listed in the previous chapter is the consequence of our disintegrated, disharmonic state. The gospel admonition to take up the cross is to do so with the same attitude that Jesus had—'and follow me'—not to go out looking for it but to have the right attitude to the inevitability of suffering and find meaning in it so that it becomes not only bearable but a positive means of advancement, a way through to freedom from it, a step towards that new life that grows out of the dying to our self-centredness. Nowhere in Scripture are we commanded to suffer. We are commanded to love. The Gospel teaches us how to handle suffering positively.

It is in the innate desire of human nature to become more, to achieve more, that we can find an explanation for the Christ-event which is more meaningful as we move into the New Age of the Spirit.

It would appear to be a characteristic of our human nature that it is always breaking new records of achievement. Why else the need for constantly updating the Guinness Book of Records? I speak here, not of achievements reached with the aid of the development of science, though that too is a human achievement, but of physical or moral achievement. It seems to be equally a characteristic of human nature that it requires the act of one human being to break through the barrier of human limitation, and once the barrier has been broken, the rest of humankind is empowered to follow through. This empowering is not a gift from without of something not already possessed. It is the liberating or release of a God-given gift already present but hitherto unused. There are plenty of examples of this in recent times.

Over the thousands of years that people have been plying between Dover and Calais it was only a hundred years ago that anyone succeeded in swimming the Channel. Once Captain Webb had done it, hundreds of others have done it, some even there and back. Recently a twelve-year-old boy did it, and within 24 hours a second boy of twelve had done it. No one had ever succeeded in reaching the summit of Mount Everest until it was reached by Hillary and his guide Tensing. Now that the barrier to human achievement has been broken, it has become almost an annual event. Recently an Italian made the ascent alone, and without oxygen. No one had ever run a mile in so short a time as four minutes. Once Bannister had succeeded in doing it, others were enabled to. For centuries people have been endeavouring to fly by their own power. Recently a young American managed to pedal a flying machine across the English Channel. Now that that particular barrier has been broken I am prepared to wager that before long we will hear of plenty of others doing the same. Enough examples.

To lift humanity out of its state of disintegration and raise it to a higher state of evolution, there needed to be one person who would break through that barrier and in doing so empower the whole of humankind to follow the same path. Jesus, of course, has been that person. He has broken through the barrier of our personal slaveries to enter a new, completely liberated life.

He was the only person who could have done this. Because he was completely human, was one of us, he was able to break through the barriers of human enslavement on our behalf. But he could only be empowered himself to do this because he was also the Christ. Only thus was he able to be completely himself, completely authentic, not coerced by any slaveries which result from our self-centredness. This is not to say that he did not take on our disintegrated condition and thereby suffer from the envies and hates and distrust and jealousies and selfishness of others, and finally from the injustice and violence which are the fruits of the disharmony of our human condition.

One thing about Jesus that shines out through the Gospel account is his complete integrity. He is a completely whole and fully integrated person. It is often said that 'he did his Father's will'. This meant that he was completely and unswervingly the person that God wanted him to be. Like us, he had been given certain talents which would make him that person and that person only, just as other talents had been withheld from him which would not have contributed to his becoming the particular person he was destined to be. Unlike us, he was undeterred by any 'outside' false self from becoming completely the 'inside' self that his Father intended him to be. He was so sure of his own value in his Father's eyes that he did not need to seek his identity along any inauthentic paths. Unlike us, he never capitulated to outside pressures.

The ultimate fear that weakens a person is the fear of death. Only the truly liberated person has no fear of death and welcomes it as the final barrier to attaining complete liberty, complete wholeness and holiness—such a state of integrity that we regard it as a 'new life', a new creation. The fear that he experienced in the Garden of Olives was caused by his foreseeing the process by which he was to die. As Jesus faced this barrier he was still 'his own man', fully in control. It was he who made the decision to pass through it: 'No one takes my life away from me. I give it up of my own free will' (Jn. 10:18). So both Matthew (27:50) and John (19:30) write of Jesus dying with the words: 'he gave up his spirit'.

There are several texts in the Epistles to describe how Jesus, by passing freely through death to new life empowers us to do the same: not only through the barrier of physical death but from the disintegrating death of personal slaveries to integral liberation. Here are a couple:

> 'For since we have become one with him in dying as he did, in the same way we shall be one with him by being raised from death and will never die again—death will no longer rule over him. In the same way you are to think of yourselves as dead, so far as sin is concerned, but living in fellowship with God through Christ Jesus' (Rom 6: 5, 8–9, 11).

> 'Since the children, as he calls them, are people of flesh and blood, Jesus himself became like them and shared their human nature. He did this so that through his death he might destroy the Devil, who has the power over death, and in this way set free those who were slaves all their lives because of their fear of death' (Heb 2: 14–15).

Because his humanity enabled him to be one with human nature he was from within, so to speak, able to raise humanity from that slavery, so that evil need no longer hold a person in bond. 'God condemned sin in human nature by sending his own Son, who came with a nature like man's sinful nature, to do away with sin' (Rom 8: 3).

We are enabled, if we wish, to have such an identity with the Christ that we are able to say with St. Paul: 'It is no longer I who live, but it is Christ who lives in me' (Gal 2:20).

These words from the Second Vatican Council seem, to my mind, to confirm this way of understanding the central truth of our Christian faith:

> 'Christ is now at work in the hearts of men through the energy of his Spirit. He arouses not only a desire for the age to come, but by that very fact, he animates, purifies, and strengthens those

noble longings too by which the human family strives to make its life more human and to render the whole earth submissive to this goal'.[9]

In Chapter Four I said that we can throw light on the way we understand God by asking ourselves how we understand sin, and ultimately by asking ourselves the question: Am I afraid of God? The reader might find it helpful, as a conclusion to this and the previous chapter to look at two contrasting columns and to ask himself or herself where he or she stands.

An anthropomorphic (humanised) concept of God	God as Being, Love, Truth
God as the angry father calling for vindictive punishment	We receive corrective punishment by having to suffer the effects of evil
Suffering and death are 'the wages of sin'.	Suffering is not in God's plan. Death is a natural event, the final letting-go on the journey to the fullness of life.
God is hurt, offended, by sin.	Sin causes us, not God, to suffer
God is our judge.	We judge ourselves when faced with the goodness of God. (Jn. 3:18)
A God who demands justice.	God the justifier—making us just.
God is to be asked to forgive us.	To be open to accept God's love *is* forgiveness.
Redemption as an act of sacrifice offered to an offended God.	The Christ-event as an empowering of humanity to become more.
Evil is that which offends God.	Evil is that which prevents growth, our own or other people's.

9. Abbott, W. GS.38.

Part Three

Our personal journey

I have been writing about the evolution of humanity's understanding of the God-humanity relationship. In this last part I consider the individual's personal journey in his/her relationship to God. This is not an intellectual journey, it is a faith journey.

11. Towards pure consciousness

The growth process is painful. Growth in our faith journey is painful because it requires us to let go of some of the deepest securities upon which we base our lives. To allow our 'faith' to be challenged is to allow growth to take place. But do we dare to allow it to be challenged?

This is the point at which the reader needs to ask whether his/her faith is in Christianity or in God and Jesus the Christ, and whether it finds its expression in practising Christianity or in living the Gospel. To put the question differently, is one motivated primarily by 'Faith', by 'a faith' or by 'the Faith'? A lot of confusion arises because these distinctions are not made.

Faith is the orientation given to life on account of the personal relationship one has with God. It provides the backdrop for all our actions, putting them into a God context. It is a grace, a gratuitious gift of God, it cannot be earned. (It takes two to build up a relationship.) It is of the heart, not the head: it is a deeply personal and abiding encounter with the transcendent. With it, God becomes a presence in one's life. Whether adverted to or not, it becomes the bed-rock of life, an uninterupted and uninterpreted transcendental experience which interprets all else. It enables an integration of all that is outside one with the deepest inside (which supposes that there is a wholeness inside with which the outside can be integrated). Its concern is Truth as an absolute, experienced through intuition, not truths as products of our intellect.

A clock provides us with an illustration. We can examine all the pieces of the machine one by one and understand how each contributes to the working of the mechanism as a whole. We can marvel at its intricacy and learn about its size and weight and the time it took to construct, but all this information will only be given a context, we will only appreciate its value as a clock, when we learn the machine's purpose: to tell the time. Our rational mind can provide us with a cosmology, an explanation of the origin and nature of our universe, but it will only become a tool of life for us, will only provide us with a satisfactory framework within which to set our lives when its purpose is illuminated by Faith.

A faith is the intuitive experience of Faith as interpreted by a particular religious tradition. If Faith tells us that life has meaning, a faith gives us a particular understanding of life's meaning that answers our needs at a given stage in our growth. It is a product of the intellect and enables us to believe in this or that mystery. It is a belief, a way of believing. It can be an interrupted or growing or decreasing experience because it is an interpreted vision. It is the servant of Faith. Having Faith we search for a faith because, being rational creatures we need to express Faith in human terms, however inadequate. A faith enables us to handle Faith in our everyday lives. Unlike the free gift of Faith, a faith can be sought after, thrashed out, and worked upon to our satisfaction, until we feel comfortable with it, which is why people change their religion or their Church.

The Faith is a series of beliefs provided by a particular religious tradition. This is a faith articulated, usually in a Creed or a set of doctrines or a catechism. Since it is subject to transmission its communication is limited by the value of the words in which it is expressed. In fact the Faith needs to be constantly re-thought and re-expressed according to each culture and time in order to remain faithful to a faith. Which is why Pope John XXIII in his address to the world's Catholic Bishops at the opening of the Second Vatican Council in 1962 said that we need 'to make a distinction between the substance of the faith (ie., the belief) and the formulas in which during the course of time it has come to be expressed' (ie., the beliefs).

This excursion into the different meanings of 'faith' has been necessary in order to make the distinction between a fundamental attitude to life and the changeable ways in which that attitude is rationalised and handled in our everyday lives.

I would suggest that direction is given to our spiritual growth from four sources: Faith (intuitive knowledge, or inner revelation), reason (rational knowledge), a particular religious tradition (a faith) with its doctrine (the Faith) to which we give our assent, and fourthly our spiritual experience, which is largely the product of the other three. All four have to be kept in balance which is why, if we are to grow spiritually, we have constantly to be re-evaluating their meaningfulness to us in the particular circumstances in which we find ourselves.

Let me illustrate this in terms of our belief in God. Our Faith accounts for our knowing God, for what God means to us in the depth of our being. But the Faith that we profess accounts for our knowing *about* God, knowledge that is the product of our rational mind, even of our imagination. One of our human limitations is our need for mental images when thinking, (and still more when communicating) about the unimaginable. As children, our imagination was lively and we used it more than we do as adults in order to form our ideas. Our first ideas about God were formed by holy pictures—varying from symbolic visual aids (the eye in the triangle) to the paintings of the great masters (an old man with a white beard)—or by bible stories or by explanations of the catechism. Try as we do, it is very difficult to shake off these early images in our adult life. No matter how much we 'intellectualise' about God, the mental pictures of our childhood lurk in the background.

I often meet people who tell me they cannot believe in God any more (often because he has not intervened miraculously to avert some human disaster) or that they have lost their faith. What I hear them saying behind the words is that their childhood picture of God no longer fits their adult understanding. The very fact of their concern about the issue implies an underlying desire to be able to relate with a God who makes sense to them. They have not lost their Faith: their trouble lies in their beliefs, which need adjusting to adulthood. Unless knowledge about God is to remain purely on the academic level—as one might put the quest to penetrate the mystery of God alongside the quest of scientists today for a Theory of the Unified Field—it must grow out of our personal experience of relating to God and how we experience his relating to us.

We cannot know God neat. We can only know God as diluted by our human condition. The God we know is a relative God: a God in relation to and in terms of our humanity. For one reason, all our knowing is within the very limited framework of our human experience. To progress in knowledge we have to proceed from the already known to the unknown, as every school teacher will affirm. New ideas, new concepts have to be hooked on to the knowledge that we have already made our own, that has become part of us. The knowledge of the peasant differs from that of the professor only because the experience of each is different. Their experience is the product of their culture and their human relationships, as much as of their education. All the outside influences on my life, good and bad, go to make up the totality of my experience. That totality is different for every person. In turn, it is upon this totality of my experience that I build my personal value system, my conscience, and this includes my religious values. What God means to me, whether he is a presence in my life or simply a notion, whether I open myself to his influence or whether I keep him at arm's length—or even deny his existence—will be decided by my conscience, depending in turn on the totality of my experience which is unique to me.

In the sense that we can only know God through and in relation to our human condition it is true to say that 'we make God to our own image and likeness' and the image will change, must change, as we change. We find it helpful to use images like the Trinity or Father or Person in relating to God but their value lies precisely in their being an aid to that relationship not in their identity with God as Absolute or as unmanifest. There is the danger that these images be given an absolute value in which case they become idols. (Witness the recent outcry when an Anglican Bishop suggested that we might equally well refer to God as 'she' rather than as 'he'!) The images become idols when they are retained on account of an intrinsic value, rather than replaced by other more useful images which nourish our evolving awareness.

What I have been offering in the previous chapters is a new imagery, a new way of thinking about some of the deepest beliefs of Christianity. I have suggested that they are more in keeping with our evolving awareness as we enter the New Age of consciousness. If we are not open to changing the imagery there is the danger that many people will 'throw the baby out with the bath water'.

The new level of awareness of our times is marked by a growing desire for transcendence, for mystical experience, for a beyond-knowing experience of God. The German theologian Karl Rahner has the facinating theory that in every human being there is this capacity for and an innate drive towards self-transcendence and that in Jesus a human being was found in whom the capacity for self-transcendence was totally realised so that he could realise himself in a total unity with God[1]. While most of us are less in tune with this innate drive, it does seem that the current evolution of consciousness, with its restoring the balance between heart and head, is enabling us to rediscover our inner-most centre, to regain our equilibrium, to find in our depth a centre of pure consciousness.

---

1. Mentioned in Weber, R. p. 173.

12. The Personal Journey into the New Age of the Spirit

From my acquaintance with Church members who are discovering the New Age of Consciousness, it appears to me that there are three stages through which such people journey. They are:

A period of awakening and wider vision;
A period of challenge and exploration;
A period of acceptance and peace

In identifying the characteristics of each stage, I am trying to record and give a sense of order to experiences as they have been recounted to me.

A period of awakening and wider vision

It starts with a sense, however vague at first, which grows into a conviction, that some big change is coming about in the world. Much bigger than any single event one hears about. It is a growing awareness that is supported by becoming more conscious of the meaning behind a lot of events and observations, all of which seem to point in one direction. They were noticed before, but not as signs of this change. They now take on a meaning; they have the same meaning.

With this new awareness of indications of some big change coming, is a parallel awareness that you are part of it. You too are changing in some way.

The coming change implies a departure from present roots, props, securities. Especially from the unchanging anchor-hold of the Church. There is a growing sense that Church teaching, and even Church life, does not ring true.

One begins to feel that the Church is not related to life as it is experienced today. There is an unreality about it. Church life seems to happen at a surface-level and not draw its life from an inner depth. Its moral teaching and its presentation of doctrine are too facile, too cut and dried, taking the human elements too little into consideration. Her teaching seems to be too rational, too left-brain, and not flow from an inner sense of Truth.

Whereas before one was content with believing in truths about God, one now begins to experience God as Truth. This causes one to have to face the question: can I go on relying solely on the Church as my source of Truth?

As this awareness develops it leads to a dark period of inner turmoil. The secure foundations are wabbling. A crisis looms ahead. Do you remain true to your growing inner conviction that Truth is experienced in the depth of your consciousness or do you remain loyal to the expressions of doctrine which no longer ring true for you?

One is faced with an inability to move back to the set pattern of one's old position: at the same time one does not have the courage to untie the mooring and launch into an uncharted sea.

With this crisis one's habitual practice of church-going and church-involvement begins to change. This leads to a sense of guilt at unfaithfulness. One is not helped by relations and friends who are quite uncomprehending and speak of 'lapsing' and 'losing your faith'.

This period continues until there comes the day that one has the courage to be true to oneself and step aside from—not necessarily out of—the institutional Church. (Later, in the third period one may step in again as a renewed person.)

What seems to be a common vehicle carrying people along this road of deepening awareness is the regular practice of some form of deep meditation or silent reflection: some exercise that turns one from a God up there or out there to discover the God in one's own still centre.

A period of challenge and exploration

With the increasing courage to let go, there comes the desire to venture out, to explore other avenues, other movements, other religions, other ideologies. One becomes a seeker. One takes the risk of involvement by reading their literature, attending their meetings, making friends with their followers.

This period of searching is a lonely one. You feel estranged from family and friends who think you are weird. They treat you with compassion as a lost sheep if they don't actually set about re-converting you.

This is a time when one desperately looks around for a counsellor; someone sympathetic with one's search with whom one can share one's thoughts and sound out one's new discoveries. This must be someone on the same wave-length who will not direct you but rather draw you out so that you enunciate what is in your unconscious mind, thus helping you to reach a free decision. One naturally thinks of priests and Religious within the Church as the sort of people who can offer guidance on this spiritual path, but sadly it is difficult to find such a guide among them. On the contrary, one is instinctively dissuaded from asking because one suspects the incomprehension with which one's tale will be met.

And yet, as one journeys, assurance and guidance come from other quarters. One gradually notices that at each step, just when the need is greatest, some person or some book or some other form of inspiration suddenly enters one's life—and often from a most unexpected source. It gives one an assurance that, after all, the Holy Spirit is there as guide along the path. An assurance for the future builds up: that when guidance is needed, guidance will be there.

Related to this is a growing sense of connectedness. One becomes increasingly aware that there is some common thread running through all the new contacts and experiences that come one's way. That somehow they are all contributing to some great movement, although that movement cannot be labelled, except to say it is the New Age or New Consciousness of which one feels one is becoming a part.

As this stage of exploration and new challenges proceeds one moves away from a desire to try to explain or defend one's journey to uncomprehending friends and family and in fact with a growing sense of relief that one is not a renegade but is being true to oneself, one becomes increasingly reluctant to try to convince others of one's new discoveries. Instead, one seeks the company of like-minded people and feels a great strength in communicating with them, albeit that this communication is often silent communication, as when a group meditates together.

Dead ends

Not all people entering the first or even the second stage go further. For one reason or another they are not able to take the courageous step required; not able to let go of those safe supports they have depended upon till now.

But then the whole of life, from self-centred babyhood, is a journey of letting go, right up to the ultimate act of surrendering ourselves to the Other in the naked passage of death. Each person makes that journey at a different pace. Not to go forward however, is to enter a dead end. To cease to grow is to diminish.

A period of acceptance and peace

The journey has been a journey inwards, to one's 'still centre', to the depth of one's consciousness. But this is not an ego-trip. It is at the same time a journey into the centre of all being, into the centre of the source of all being, all life, all love, into the wholeness (holiness) of God. There one discovers the world and all creation and all people anew.

One experiences a unity with all life. One finds that one is relating to all creation and especially to other people in a new way. The God-life within oneself recognises its unity with the God-life in others to the extent that one feels that they and oneself are part of a whole.

This causes a growth in concern for the suffering, the needy, for ecology, for mending and healing and making whole. It brings about a desire to break down the barriers people erect to keep themselves apart, disintegrated. One promotes peace. One's sense of justice is sharpened. One recognises the good in all things; the good even in the official enemies.

One appreciates the good and the truth and the sincerity found in other religions. One recognises that they are all paths, blessed by God, to lead people to the ultimate Truth. One intuitively feels that the different religions are simply parts of a whole, a total ascent of humankind to God, and that one day the differences between them will become insignificant compared with the unity of consciousness that already unites humanity.

One's search for Truth is replacing one's former reliance on truths. The different and imperfect expressions of truths diminish in importance. One is gradually relying more upon the truth of one's own experience. An inner authority stemming from the truth of experience replaces the need to surrender to an outside authoirty.

With the growing acceptance that one's path, though often far from clear, is absolutely right and true, comes a great inner peace. One experiences that richness lies within, in the quality of life, and one is attracted to a more simple lifestyle. This is one expression of one's new found liberation and it is accompanied by a deeper inner joy. Without feeling the need to communicate this verbally to people one feels that just by being that sort of person one affects others around and in this way brings about the New Age in our midst.

Conclusion

As we approach the new millennium, we live in an exciting time: a time of great new possibilities.

Over the millions of years during which creation has evolved—from matter to plants to animals to human beings—the evolutionary thrust has been passive, deterministic. The process has taken place without being a conscious development, without any choice being made on the part of the subjects of change. The next great step, the evolution of consciousness, by the very fact of its self-reflective nature, is of a different order. It can come about only because it is willed: because humanity, acting with freedom and deliberation, chooses to co-operate with the divine creative energy to bring about maximum consciousness, the *Omega* point.

Teilhard de Chardin names two conditions for this point to be reached. The first is that we be on our guard against the pessimism and despondency that might cause us to recoil from the effort required to promote this break-through. Any retreat from the negativity of our world into a life-style which is a flight from its reality, or indeed any harbouring of negative thoughts about humanity's future, can only be an obstacle to the free flow of God's creative energy. The second condition, the very reverse of the first, is that we commit ourselves to positive action to promote the evolutionary process.

We have not only to believe in its possibility, but to utter with deepest conviction, that plea we make each time we say the Lord's Prayer: 'Thy Kingdom *come*, thy will be done *on earth* as it is in heaven. . . .'.

This conviction calls us to be more loving towards our world and towards all humanity, since the *Omega* point is also the climax and crown of universal love, the fulfilment of the Kingdom. We have to summon all the energies of which we are capable to promote and foster unity and love, the great constructive forces of the future.

This requires us to understand the *Omega* point not simply as the climax of a biological process, nor even as the final goal of the human condition, but as Someone, a person on whom our human love is focussed; the Christ, in whom and through whom total unity will be achieved.

I conclude with words of Teilhard de Chardin which were echoed by the world's two thousand Catholic Bishops at the Second Vatican Council:

'The future of humanity lies in the hands of those who are strong enough to provide coming generations with reasons for living and hoping'[1]

[1]Abbott, w. GS31.

References

Abbott, W. (Ed.). *The Documents of Vatican II*. Geoffrey Chapman, London, 1966.
LG = 'The Church'.
GS = 'The Church in the Modern World'.
DH = 'Religious Freedom'.
NA = Relationship of the Church to non-Christian Religions.
Aron, E & A. *The Maharishi Effect*. Stillpoint Publishing, New Hampshire, USA. 1986.
Assagioli, Roberto. *The Act of Will*. Turnstone Press Ltd. Wellingborough, England. 1984.
Balasuriya, T. *Planetary Theology*. SCM Press, London. 1984.
Barnaby, Frank. (Ed.). *The Gaia Peace Atlas*. Pan Books, London. 1988.
Baum, Gregory. *Man Becoming*. Herder and Herder, New York. 1970.
Berry, Thomas. *Contemplation and World Order*. Riverdale Papers V. Riverdale Centre for Religious Research, New York.
Brooke, Anthony. *The Awakening of Man*. A lecture published in 'Findhorn News'. Sept. 1973, The Findhorn Press, Forres, IV36 OTZ.
Brueggemann, Walter. *The Prophetic Imaginaiton*. Fortress Press, Philadelphia. 1978.
Bühlmann, Walbert. *The Chosen Peoples*. St. Paul Publications, Slough, England. 1982.
Campbell, Anthony. *Seven States of Consciousness*. Victor Gallancz Ltd., London. 1974.
Capra, Fritjof. *The Turning Point*. Fontana Paperbacks, London. 1982.
Cohen, J.M. and Phipps J.F. *The Common Experience*. Rider & Co., London. 1979.
Cuming, K.G. *God and the New Age*. A Michael Link Publication. 1975.
Cupitt, Don. *The World to Come*. SCM Press, London. 1982.
Life Lines. SCM Press, London 1986.
Davies, Paul. *God and the New Physics*. Penguin Books, London. 1984.
(EN) *Evangelisation in the Modern World*. Pope Paul VI. CTS Edition, London. 1975.
Ferguson, Marilyn. *The Aquarian Conspiracy*. Paladin, Granada, London. 1982.
Fox, Matthew. *Original Blessing*. Bear & Co., Santa Fe, New Mexico, USA. 1983.
Griffiths, Bede. *Return to the Centre*. Fount Paperback, London. 1978.
Haag, H. *Is Original Sin in the Scripture?* Sheed & Ward, London. 1969.
Happold, F.C. *Religious Faith and Twentieth Century Man*. DLT, London. 1980.
Hay, David. *Exploring Inner Space*. Penguin Books, London. 1982.
Heisenberg, Werner. *Physics and Philosophy*. Harper Torchbooks, New York. 1958.
Hick, John and Knitter, Paul. (Eds). *The Myth of Christian Uniqueness*. SCM Press, London. 1988.
Huxley, Julian. A lecture delivered in New York and published in the *Scientific Monthly*, 1940.
Knitter, P.F. *No Other Name?* SCM Press, London. 1985.

Kuhn, Thomas. *The Structure of Scientific Revolutions*, The University of Chicago Press, 1962.
Lipnack, J and Stamps, J. *The Networking Book*. Routledge & Kegan Paul, London. 1986.
Lonergan, A and Richards, C. *Thomas Berry and the New Cosmology*. Twenty-Third Publications, CT, USA. 1987.
Lovelock, James. *Gaia: A New Look at Life on Earth*. OUP. 1979.
Merton, Thomas. *Conjectures of a Guilty Bystander*. Doubleday, New York. 1968.
Murphy-O'Connor. J. *Becoming Human Together*. Veritas, Dublin. 1978.
Myers, Norman. *The Gaia Atlas of Planet Management*. Pan Books, London. 1985.
MacGregor, G. *Gnosis: A Renaissance in Christian Thought*. A Quest Book, Wheaton, Illinois, USA. 1979.
MacNulty, K. *UK Social Change through a wide-angle lens*. Article in Futures Journal, August 1985, Butterworth Scientific Ltd., Guildford, based on Monitor programme's annual survey.
Macquarrie, John. *Principles of Christian Theology*. SCM Press, London 1979.
O'Brien, A. 'Sin, Centre and Self'. An article in *TM: An Aid to Christian Growth*. McCrimmon, Great Wakering, GB. 1983.
Ó Murchú, D. *The God Who Becomes Redundant*. Mercier Press, Cork. 1986. *Coping with Change in the Modern World*. Mercier Press, Cork. 1987.
Paton, D.M. (Ed.). *Breaking Barriers: Nairobi 1975*. SPCK, London. 1976.
Peck, M.Scott. *People of the Lie*. Century Hutchinson, London. 1983.
Populorum Progressio. The encyclical letter of Pope Paul VI on 'The Development of Peoples'. 1967. CTS, London.
Robertson, J. *The Sane Alternative: A Choice of Futures*. Published by the Author. 1983.
Robinson, Bishop John. *Honest to God*. SCM Press, London. 1963.
Russell, Peter. *The Awakening Earth*. Routledge & Kegan Paul, London. 1982.
Schillebeeckx E. 'Christian Faith and the Future of the World' in *The Church Today*.
Schuon, F. *The Transcendent Unity of Religions*. Harper & Row, New York. 1975.
Sheehan, Thomas. *The First Coming*. The Aquarian Press, Wellingborough, 1988.
Sheldrake, Rupert. *A New Science of Life*. Paladin, London. 1983.
Smith, Adrian B. *A Reason for Hope: The Human Experience of the Kingdom of God*. McCrimmon, Great Wakering, Essex. 1986.
Spink, Canon Peter. *Spiritual Man in a New Age*. DLT, London. 1980.
Teilhard de Chardin, P. 'The Formation of the Noosphere', a paper of 1947 published in the *The Future of Man*. Collins, London. 1964.
Tillich, Paul. *The Courage to be*. Fontana, London, 1962.
Toffler, Alvin. *Future Shock*. Pan Books, London. 1970. *The Third Wave*. Pan Books, London. 1981.
Toynbee, A. *A Study of History*.
Trevelyan, Sir George. *A Vision of the Aquarian Age*. Coventure Ltd., London. 1977.
Verney, Bishop Stephen. *Into the New Age*. Fontana, London. 1976.
Watson, Lyall. *Lifetide*. Hodder and Stoughton, London. 1979. *Suepernature II*. Hodder and Stoughton, London. 1987.
Weber, Renée. *Dialogue with Scientists and Sages*. Routledge and Kegan Paul, London. 1986.
Weiderkehr, Dietrich. *Belief in Redemption*. SPCK, London. 1979.
Wijngaards, John. *God Within Us*. Collins Fount Paperback, London. 1988.
Wilber, Ken. *Up from Eden*. Routledge & Kegan Paul, London. 1983.
Wojtyla, Karol. *Sources of Renewal*. Collins Fount Paperback, London. 1980.

Acknowledgements

Grateful acknowledgement is made for permission to reprint:

Two drawings (on pages 58 and 60) provided by Rupert Sheldrake, used in his 1984 'Tomorrow's World' TV programme.

Extracts from two books, 'The God Who Becomes Redundant' and 'Coping with Change in the Modern World' by Diarmuid Ó Murchú.

A table (on page 63) from 'The Sane Alternative' (revised edition 1983) published by the author, James Robertson.

Extracts from the English translation of the papal documents 'Dominum et Vivificantem' and 'Evangelii Nuntiandi' published by the Catholic Truth Society, London.

A passage from Peter Spink's book 'Spiritual Man in a New Age'.

A quotation from 'One Earth', the magazine of The Findhorn Foundation, The Park, Findhorn, Forres, IV36 OTZ, Scotland.

Two excerpts from 'Gnosis' by Geddes MacGregor, © 1979 Geddes MacGregor, reprinted by permission of the publisher, The Theosophical Publishing House, Wheaton, Illinios, USA.

A passage from Lyall Watson's 'Lifetide', published by Hodder and Stoughton, 1979.

Selected quotations from 'The Documents of Vatican II' edited by Walter Abbott, 1966, published in UK by Geoffrey Chapman (Cassell).

Short extracts from Tissa Balasuriya's 'Planetary Theology' (1984) and John Macquarrie's 'Principles of Christian Theology' (1979) both published by SCM Press.

Two short quotations from 'Is Original Sin in the Scripture?' by Herbert Haag published by Sheed & Ward Ltd., London (1969).

Selected brief quotations from 'Belief in Redemption' by D. Wiederkehr, translated by Jeremy Moiser. Translation © SPCK/John Knox Press, 1979.

Short quotations from 'The Future of Man' by P. Teilhard de Chardin, published by William Collins, London, 1964.

A passage from 'Sources of Renewal' by Karol Wojtyla, Fount Paper-back, 1980.

Three brief quotations from 'A Vision of the Aquarian Age' by Sir George Trevelyan (1977).

For Further Reading

If you have enjoyed this book, you will also enjoy reading the author's previous book

A Reason For Hope:
The Human Experience of the Kingdom of God

in which he shows that the Kingdom, and not the Church, was at the centre of Jesus' preaching, and the implications of that message for life in our present world.

What people have said about it:

This is one of the most exciting books I have read in a long time . . . I will certainly make use of it in my programmes of adult religious education.

Rev. Michael Austin S.J.
R.E. Director, Cape Town.

I have read 'A Reason for Hope' twice and I am profoundly grateful. This is because I find hope much more difficult to foster than faith or love. This book has helped me more than any other I have read recently.

Theo Westow, a theologian

Congratulations and thanks for 'A Reason for Hope'. You take what has been seen before, but bring new insights, point out correlations and developments, and project into the future. This is what most people can't do, and what only few pastoral planners accomplish in a language so understandable as yours.

Dr. Robert Delaney,
Franciscan Communications,
Los Angeles

Definitely required reading for all those seriously engaged in mission. An exciting vision not of where we are going, but of where we are now if only we have eyes to see and ears to hear.

Father Joe Brankin,
General Secretary, National
Missionary Council for
England and Wales

Available from leading bookshops or direct from the publisher, £2.95 + 50p, p&p. McCrimmon Publishing Co. Ltd., 10-12 High Street, Great Wakering, Essex, SS3 OEQ, U.K.